Machine Learning for VLSI Chip Design

Scrivener Publishing
100 Cummings Center, Suite 541J
Beverly, MA 01915-6106

Publishers at Scrivener
Martin Scrivener (martin@scrivenerpublishing.com)
Phillip Carmical (pcarmical@scrivenerpublishing.com)

Machine Learning
for VLSI Chip Design

Edited by
Abhishek Kumar
Suman Lata Tripathi
and
K. Srinivasa Rao

Scrivener
Publishing

WILEY

This edition first published 2023 by John Wiley & Sons, Inc., 111 River Street, Hoboken, NJ 07030, USA and Scrivener Publishing LLC, 100 Cummings Center, Suite 541J, Beverly, MA 01915, USA
© 2023 Scrivener Publishing LLC
For more information about Scrivener publications please visit www.scrivenerpublishing.com.

Wiley Global Headquarters
111 River Street, Hoboken, NJ 07030, USA

For details of our global editorial offices, customer services, and more information about Wiley products visit us at www.wiley.com.

Library of Congress Cataloging-in-Publication Data

ISBN 9781119910398

Front cover images supplied by Pixabay.com
Cover design by Russell Richardson

Set in size of 11pt and Minion Pro by Manila Typesetting Company, Makati, Philippines

Printed in the USA

10 9 8 7 6 5 4 3 2 1

Contents

List of Contributors

Imran Ullah Khan
Dept. of Electronics and Communication Engineering, Integral University, Lucknow, India

Nupur Mittal
Dept. of Electronics and Communication Engineering, Integral University, Lucknow, India

Mohd. Amir Ansari
Dept. of Electronics and Communication Engineering, Integral University, Lucknow, India

A.V. Ananthalakshmi
Department of ECE, Puducherry Technological University, Puducherry, India

P. Divyaparameswari
Department of ECE, Puducherry Technological University, Puducherry, India

P. Kanimozhi
Department of ECE, Puducherry Technological University, Puducherry, India

Jyoti Kandpal
Dept. of Electronics and Communication Engineering, NIT Arunanchal Pradesh, India

Rajeswari
Department of ECE, Lakireddy Bali Reddy College of Engineering, Mylavaram, India

N. Vinod Kumar
Department of ECE, Lakireddy Bali Reddy College of Engineering, Mylavaram, India

K. M. Suresh
Department of ECE, Lakireddy Bali Reddy College of Engineering, Mylavaram, India

N. Sai Kumar
Department of ECE, Lakireddy Bali Reddy College of Engineering, Mylavaram, India

K. Girija Sravani
Department of ECE, KL University, Green Fields, Guntur-522502, Andhra Pradesh, India

P. Kiran Kumar
Koneru Lakshmaiah Educational Foundation (Deemed to be University), Guntur, Andhra Pradesh-522502, India

B. Balaji
Koneru Lakshmaiah Educational Foundation (Deemed to be University), Guntur, Andhra Pradesh-522502, India

M. Suman
Koneru Lakshmaiah Educational Foundation (Deemed to be University), Guntur, Andhra Pradesh-522502, India

P. Syam Sundar
Koneru Lakshmaiah Educational Foundation (Deemed to be University), Guntur, Andhra Pradesh-522502, India

E. Padmaja
Koneru Lakshmaiah Educational Foundation (Deemed to be University), Guntur, Andhra Pradesh-522502, India

Ritu Yadav
ECE Department, I K Gujaral Punjab Technical University, Jalandhar, India

Kiran Ahuja
ECE Department, DAVIET, Jalandhar, India

K. Sasi Bhushan
Department of Electronics and Communication Engineering, Lakireddy Bali Reddy College of Engineering (Autonomous), Mylavaram, Krishna District, AP, India, 521230

U. Preethi
Department of Electronics and Communication Engineering, Lakireddy Bali Reddy College of Engineering (Autonomous), Mylavaram, Krishna District, AP, India, 521230

P. Naga Sai Navya
Department of Electronics and Communication Engineering, Lakireddy Bali Reddy College of Engineering (Autonomous), Mylavaram, Krishna District, AP, India, 521230

R. Abhilash
Department of Electronics and Communication Engineering, Lakireddy Bali Reddy College of Engineering (Autonomous), Mylavaram, Krishna District, AP, India, 521230

T. Pavan
Department of Electronics and Communication Engineering, Lakireddy Bali Reddy College of Engineering (Autonomous), Mylavaram, Krishna District, AP, India, 521230

B. Ramesh Reddy
Department of Electronics and Communication Engineering, LBR College of Engineering, Mylavaram, Krishna District, Andhra Pradesh

K. Bhargav Manikanta
Department of Electronics and Communication Engineering, LBR College of Engineering, Mylavaram, Krishna District, Andhra Pradesh

P.V.V.N.S. Jaya Sai
Department of Electronics and Communication Engineering, LBR College of Engineering, Mylavaram, Krishna District, Andhra Pradesh

R. Mohan Chandra
Department of Electronics and Communication Engineering, LBR College of Engineering, Mylavaram, Krishna District, Andhra Pradesh

M. Greeshma Vyas
Department of Electronics and Communication Engineering, LBR College of Engineering, Mylavaram, Krishna District, Andhra Pradesh

B. V. Anil Sai Kumar
School of Electronics and Electrical Engineering, Lovely Professional University, Punjab, India

Suryavamsham Prem Kumar
School of Electronics and Electrical Engineering, Lovely Professional University, Punjab, India

Konduru Jaswanth
School of Electronics and Electrical Engineering, Lovely Professional University, Punjab, India

Kola Vishnu
School of Electronics and Electrical Engineering, Lovely Professional University, Punjab, India

Abhishek Kumar
School of Electronics and Electrical Engineering, Lovely Professional University, Punjab, India

Narendra Babu Alur
Department of Electronics and Communication Engineering, and Engineering, Lakireddy Bali Reddy College of Engineering (Autonomous), Mylavaram, Krishna District, AP, India

Kurapati Poorna Durga
Department of Electronics and Communication Engineering, and Engineering, Lakireddy Bali Reddy College of Engineering (Autonomous), Mylavaram, Krishna District, AP, India

Boddu Ganesh
Department of Electronics and Communication Engineering, and Engineering, Lakireddy Bali Reddy College of Engineering (Autonomous), Mylavaram, Krishna District, AP, India

Manda Devakaruna
Department of Electronics and Communication Engineering, and Engineering, Lakireddy Bali Reddy College of Engineering (Autonomous), Mylavaram, Krishna District, AP, India

Lakkimsetti Nandini
Department of Electronics and Communication Engineering, and Engineering, Lakireddy Bali Reddy College of Engineering (Autonomous), Mylavaram, Krishna District, AP, India

A. Praneetha
Department of Computer Science Engineering, Lakireddy Bali Reddy College of Engineering (Autonomous), Mylavaram, Krishna District, AP, India

T. Satyanarayana
Department of Electronics and Communication Engineering, and Engineering, Lakireddy Bali Reddy College of Engineering (Autonomous), Mylavaram, Krishna District, AP, India

K. Rani Rudrama
Department of Electronics and Communication Engineering, Lakireddy Bali Reddy College of Engineering (Autonomous), Mylavaram, Krishna District, AP, India

Mounika Ramala
Department of Electronics and Communication Engineering, Lakireddy Bali Reddy College of Engineering (Autonomous), Mylavaram, Krishna District, AP, India

Poorna sasank Galaparti
Department of Electronics and Communication Engineering, Lakireddy Bali Reddy College of Engineering (Autonomous), Mylavaram, Krishna District, AP, India

Manikanta Chary Darla
Department of Electronics and Communication Engineering, Lakireddy Bali Reddy College of Engineering (Autonomous), Mylavaram, Krishna District, AP, India

Siva Sai Prasad Loya
Department of Electronics and Communication Engineering, Lakireddy Bali Reddy College of Engineering (Autonomous), Mylavaram, Krishna District, AP, India

K. Srinivasa Rao
Department of Electronics and Communication Engineering, KLEF, Vaddeswaram, Green Fields, 522502, Andhra Pradesh, India

T. Anil Raju
Department of Electronics and Communication Engineering, Lakireddy Bali Reddy College of Engineering, Mylavaram

K. Srihari Reddy
Department of Electronics and Communication Engineering, Lakireddy Bali Reddy College of Engineering, Mylavaram

Sk. Arifulla Rabbani
Department of Electronics and Communication Engineering, Lakireddy Bali Reddy College of Engineering, Mylavaram

G. Suresh
Department of Electronics and Communication Engineering, Lakireddy Bali Reddy College of Engineering, Mylavaram

K. Saikumar Reddy
Department of Electronics and Communication Engineering, Lakireddy Bali Reddy College of Engineering, Mylavaram

Rajesh C. Dharmik
Department of Information Technology, Yeshwantrao Chavan College of Engineering, Nagpur

Bhushan U. Bawankar
Department of Information Technology, Yeshwantrao Chavan College of Engineering, Nagpur

Preface

Machine Learning (ML) has touched all corners of human life and industry. Databased learning intelligence supports are the scalability of present technology and architecture. The current ML and deep learning (DL) algorithms require huge consumption of data and power. The industry is looking for an efficient VLSI circuit that can meet the demands of the AI-ML-DL universe. ML can pioneer different sectors throughout design methodologies from RTL design, synthesis, and verification. One of the deepest challenges of chip design is the time-consuming iterative process. Thanks to the learning model, time is considerably reduced. VLSI-based solutions and innovation of AI-ML-DL applications are growing in demand. Internet of Things–based solutions address the various challenges in society that require chips. This new book covers the latest AI/ML techniques, VLSI chip design, and systems to address societal challenges.

Applications of VLSI Design in Artificial Intelligence and Machine Learning

Imran Ullah Khan, Nupur Mittal* and Mohd. Amir Ansari

Dept. of Electronics and Communication Engineering, Integral University,
Lucknow, India

Abstract

In our advanced times, complementary metal-oxide semiconductor (CMOS) based organizations like semiconductor and gadgets face extreme scheduling of products and other different pressures. For resolving this issue, electronic design automation (EDA) must provide "design-based equivalent scaling" to continue the critical industry trajectory. For solving this problem machine learning techniques should be used both inside and "peripherally" in the design tools and flows. This article reviews machine learning opportunities, and physical implementation of IC will also be discussed. Cloud intelligence-enabled machine learning-based data analytics has surpassed the scalability of current computing technologies and architectures. The current methods based on deep learning are inefficient, require a lot of data and power consumption, and run on a data server with a long delay. With the advent of self-driving cars, unmanned aerial vehicles and robotics, there is a huge need to analyze only the necessary sensory data with low latency and low power consumption on edge devices. In this discussion, we will talk about effective AI calculations, for example, fast least squares, binary and tensor convolutional neural organization techniques, and compare prototype accelerators created in field preogrammable gate array (FPGA) and CMOS-ASIC chips. Planning on future resistive random access memory (RRAM) gadgets will likewise be briefly depicted.

Keywords: VLSI, AI, ML, CAD & AVM

---

*Corresponding author: mittal@iul.ac.in

Abhishek Kumar, Suman Lata Tripathi, and K. Srinivasa Rao (eds.) Machine Learning for VLSI Chip Design, (1–18) © 2023 Scrivener Publishing LLC

1.1 Introduction

Rapid growth in IC technology is catching up with IC design capabilities, mainly due to the significant advancement in artificial intelligence. The computational tasks assigned to very large-scale integration (VLSI) are time-consuming processes but when AI is implemented to perform the same computational tasks, the required time will be reduced. As technology advances rapidly, VLSI developers must observe and implement this growth to augment design tools. Improved design methods, features, and capabilities bring the promise of AI to VLSI design. Although artificial intelligence brings many features and methods, it still has certain limitations to bring solutions to various problems. As a result, the advent of machine learning (ML) opens up a slew of new possibilities for collaboration and particular sectors of VLSI and computer-based design. By using AI, chips are designed and implemented. It is seen as the premier application of artificial intelligence. Currently, computer-based design tools are commonly utilised in conjunction with information learned from introductory AI classes. Previously, chips were mostly hand-designed, the chip size was too large, and the performance was slow. Validating those chips based on hand-designed designs is a complex task. These complexities lead to the development of automated tools. The automation tool has been upgraded for other tasks assigned to it. Researchers bring new design methods from time to time, such as memory combinations, new programs in computing tasks, etc., in the design process, which must be mechanised. For these objectives, companies such as Intel, IBM, and others have in-house computer-aided design (CAD) capabilities [1–4]. Cadence, Synopsys, Mentor Graphics, and a slew of other companies sell CAD software, which can be thought of as artificial intelligence applied to chip design. For identifying patterns, documents retrieved or gathered from clusters is sometimes required. Such patterns can be detected by concentrating on things like classifying diverse items, forecasting points of interest, input-output linkages based on their complexity, and deep neural networks with numerous other layers for each pattern, object, and speech recognition application. In the domains mentioned above, technology is of tremendous importance. DNNs must respond to new information by comparing it to previously proposed information or procedures. This has to be expanded to the most recent development level. If the system is non-stationary, the decision-making process must be tweaked in order to enhance the increasing efficiency, which is a result of machine learning [5, 6].

In former times, huge computers made up of large-size vaccum tubes were used. Even though they were heralded as the world's fastest computers at the time, they were no match for current machines. With each passing second, modern computers become smaller, faster, cheaper, more powerful, and more efficient. But what is causing this shift? With the introduction of Bardeen's (1947–48) semiconductor transistor and Shockley's (1949) bipolar transistor at Bell Labs, the entire computing field entered a new era of electronic downsizing. The development span of microelectronics is shorter than the average human lifespan, but it has seen as many as four generations. Small-scale integration (SSI) was a term used in the early 1960s to describe low-density manufacturing procedures in which the number of transistors was restricted to roughly ten.

In the late 1960s, this gave way to Medium-Scale Integration (MSI), which allowed for the placement of roughly 100 transistors on a single chip. The Transistor-Transistor Logic (TTL), which provided higher integration densities, outlasted other IC families' Emitter-Coupled Logic (ECL) and established the foundation for integrated circuit uprising. Texas Instruments, Fairchild, Motorola, and National Semiconductor all trace their roots back to the establishment of this family. The development of transistor counts to roughly 1,000 per chip, known as large-scale integration, began in the early 1970s (LSI). On a single chip the number of transistors had surpassed 1,000 by the mid-1980s, ushering in the era of very high-scale integration (VLSI). Despite the fact that significant advances have been achieved and transistor counts have increased, TTL was vanquished in the struggle against the MOS at this time, due to the same concerns that put the vacuum tube out of commission: power consumption and the number of gates that could be placed on a single die. With the introduction of the microprocessors, Intel's 4004 in 1972 and the 8080 in 1974, the second period of the integrated circuit revolution began. Texas Instruments, Infineon, Alliance Semiconductors, Cadence, Synopsys, Cisco, Micron, National Semiconductor, STMicroelectronics, Qualcomm, Lucent, Mentor Graphics, Analog Devices, Intel, Philips, Motorola, and many others are among the firms that make semiconductors today. Many aspects of VLSI have been demonstrated and committed to, including programmable logic devices (PLDs), hardware languages, design tools, embedded systems, and so on. As an example, the creation of an artificial neural network necessitates the use of several neural hubs as well as various amplifiers stages. With an increase in the number of neural hubs, a larger area is required to position such nodes, and the number of neural node interdependencies in diverse layers appears to be modest. It complicates cell networking in a small chip zone; therefore big area specifications for speakers and storage devices limit the device's volume. Due to the device's unpredictable nature, using a fuzzy logic chip with a large number of information sources is impractical.

1.2   Artificial Intelligence

Artificial intelligence is a branch of computer emphasis on invention of technology that can engage in intelligent actions. Humans have been fascinated by the ability to construct sentient robots since ancient times, and today, thanks to the introduction of computers and 50 years of scientific research into machine intelligence development tools, that dream is becoming a reality. Researchers are developing computers that can think like humans, interpret speech, defeat human chess grandmasters, and perform a slew of other previously unimaginable tasks [2].

1.3   Artificial Intelligence & VLSI (AI and VLSI)

The field of expert systems functioning as design assistants is where artificial intelligence (AI) is thriving in silicon chip and printed circuit design schematics [3, 9]. However, AI is simply one facet of expert technology. VLSI designing is a difficult task. That complexity is also multi-dimensional. Self-design and the patterned origin of the construction process are two others. AI language aids in the resolution of such difficult issues. These language properties, when joined with intelligent systems, enable a critical first step in addressing extremely difficult issues, notably confirming the design's validity [3].

1.4   Applications of AI

Uses of AI are developing quickly. These are being sought after in college research as well as in modern conditions like in industries. The field of VLSI design is adapting AI rapidly [7, 8, 11]. The first important application is the expert system, an intelligent computer software that mimics the behaviour of a human by employing analytical techniques to a specific domain's knowledge base. Expert systems in the professional field should be capable of resolving instant and reasonably challenging situations. Each difficulty should have one or even more solutions provided by an expert system. These alternatives should be reliable. Expert systems differ from regular computer programs in several important ways. "Intelligence" is specifically written into the code of traditional computer programmes. The code subsequently fixes the issue by using a well-known algorithm to do so. The "intelligence" part of expert systems is distinct from the controlling or reasoning part. Modification and improvements to the learning can be made without affecting the control portion [4]. The key aspect of artificial intelligence's knowledge-based techniques is that they ask human specialists what knowledge they use to solve certain tasks and then design multiple algorithms formats that can directly express that information. Researchers that have used this technology in a variety of VLSI applications have seen some advantages over simpler methods., such as those discussed in [4].

Making incremental improvements will be easier by using this method and it is easier for the system to describe what it is doing and why. For human experts it is easy to identify where the system's knowledge is incorrect or incomplete and describe how to solve it. It is easier to interact with human professionals' abilities.

In VLSI design these expert system are being used widely [7, 8, 10, 12]. Design Automation Assistant (DAA) was one of the first expertise solutions for VLSI design. In VLSI, it is very crucial. Researchers from Carnegie-Mellon University and AT&T Bell Labs collaborated to create it. The original DAA had rules describing several synthesis activities. Registers, operators, data routes, and control signals were used to represent production rules. Over the years, the DAA technology has been continually improved and expanded [3]. Its database contains over 500 rules that are utilised in the construction of various systems. NCR's Design Advisor serves as a professional help. The design advisor's job is to offer guidance in six areas for the creation of semi-custom CMOS devices using a library of functional blocks. Simulations, functions, timing, testability, design rules, and specification feasibility are all covered in the advisor.

1.5   Machine Learning

Advanced systems are being used and developed that are capable of learning and adapting without explicit instructions by analysing and drawing inferences from data patterns utilising specific algorithms models [13]. Machine learning also includes Artificial intelligence. Machine learning covers a vast area in medicine, email filtering, speech recognition, and computer vision. For many uses, developing traditional algo is not possible. The solution is machine learning [14–16]. The use of machine learning in biological datasets is on the rise.

Computation analytics, which emphasizes the use of computers to generate predictions, is closely related to machine learning; however, not all algorithms are statistical learning. Unsupervised learning is the focus of data mining, which is a similar topic of research. Biological brains is also a very important application of machine learning [17, 18].

1.6   Applications of ML

1.6.1   Role of ML in Manufacturing Process

A manufacturer can gain actual benefits with the use of ML, such as increased efficiency and lower costs. Machine learning can be used to improve the industry sector. In the case of Google, the company reduced its data center electricity usage by 40% by using custom ML. Google also tried to reduce it manually but that improvement was not acheived. Many other companies adopted ML. Using machine learning to improve internal operational efficiency, more than 80% say it helps them reduce costs.

1.6.2   Reducing Maintenance Costs and Improving Reliability

Machine learning can be used to create optimized maintenance schedules based on actual equipment usage. In the same way, customers will also benefit, since they can be offered personalized maintenance plans.

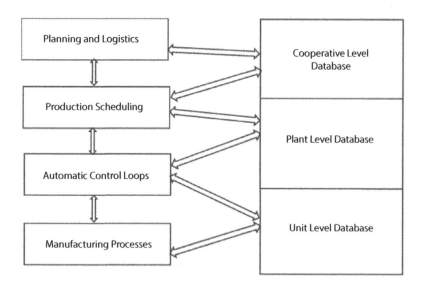

Figure 1.1 Machine learning in process industries.

Using machine learning to more accurately predict customer demand, a textile manufacturer was able to reduce inventory levels by 30%. By using ML, inventory levels and waste can also be reduced.

1.6.3   Enhancing New Design

With the help of ML, the consumer exactly knows the application of the product. If the product fails, anyone can know the reason behind it. These problems can be fed back to the team, which will remove all the problems with the help of machine learning. By using ML researchers can enhance their R&D capabilities. Figure 1.1 shows the hierarchical applications of data analytics and machine learning in process industries.

1.7   Role of ML in Mask Synthesis

Various resolution enhancement techniques (RET), such as optical proximity correction (OPC), source mask co-optimization, and sub-resolution assist functions (SRAF), become necessary as technological nodes reach the limits of optical wavelengths. Machine learning will be used by various RETs to improve mask synthesis turnaround time.

Figure 1.2 provides a structured mask synthesize flow in which source patterns (layout) are given and mask patterns are created after iterative optimization techniques such as SRAF generation, OPC, mask rule check (MRC), and lithography compliance check (LCC) [19]. A sub-resolution help function is included in SRAF generation to make target pattern printing easier. The target pattern's edge part is tailored for robust lithography in OPC. Mask manufacturing rules should be reviewed following these optimization techniques in MRC to assure mask fabrication friendliness. In Figure 1.3 to correct for image imperfections brought on by diffraction or other process effects,

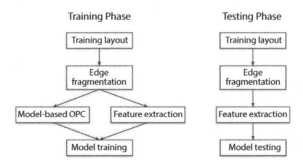

Figure 1.2 Machine learning–based optical proximity correction flow [20].

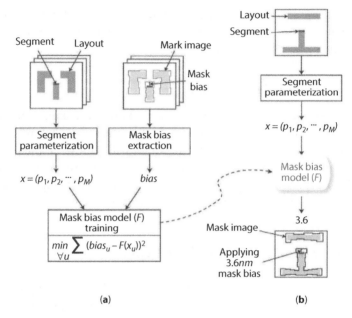

Figure 1.3 Optical proximity correction [21].

photolithography enhancement techniques like optical proximity correction (OPC) are frequently used. Due to the limits of light, OPC is mostly required in the production of semiconductor devices in order to maintain the edge placement integrity of the original design after processing into the etched image on the silicon wafer. Inconsistencies in the projected images, such as lines that are larger or thinner than intended, can be corrected by altering the pattern on the photomask used for imaging to test printability. LCC runs lithography simulation under such a series of process windows.

As illustrated in Figure 1.2, varied focus and dosage conditions are used to develop printed contours, such as minimal, inner, and outer contours (b). Two metrics are presented to evaluate the methods; in particular, the spacing between the target pattern profile and the nominal profile is measured by Edge Placement Error (EPE), while the area between the inner and outer profiles is measured by Process Variation (PV) Band. Minimizing the EPE and PV bands is a common RET goal. The flow of machine learning–based optical proximity correction and how optical proximity correction is produced are depicted in Figures 1.2 and 1.3.

1.8 Applications in Physical Design

This part will incorporate a few critical utilizations of pattern matching and AI in physical design (counting physical verification).

1.8.1   Lithography Hotspot Detection

A hotspot has been located by hotspot detection problem on a given layout with quick turnaround time. Pattern images using complicated lithography models have been obtained using conventional lithography simulation [22]. In spite of the fact that it is exact, full-chip lithography simulation is computationally costly and, in this way, we cannot give quick criticism to direct early physical design stages. Area of hotspot identification assumes a significant part in spanning the immense role among modeling and process aware physical design. A great deal of machine learning–based hotspot identification works. Machine learning methods build a relapse model in light of a bunch of preparing information. This strategy can normally recognize a past obscure hotspot. Be that as it may, it might produce a false alarm, and the hotspot recognized is not a genuine one. Step-by-step instructions to further develop the recognizing precision is the principal challenge while taking on machine learning methods. Numerous new methodologies use support vector machines (SVM) and artificial neural network (ANN) strategies to develop the hotspot discovery kernel. In [23], 2D distance change and histogram extraction on pixel-based design pictures for building SVM-based hotspot recognition are examined.

1.8.2   Pattern Matching Approach

In hotspot identification, design matching-based techniques are also commonly used. [23] proposes a format diagram to represent pattern-related CD variety. Hotspots such as closed highlights, L-shaped pieces, and complex examples can be observed using the result graphic. Range design [24] is proposed to condense process-subordinate particulars, and [25] is improved to accommodate new types of hotspot. A reach design is a 2-D format of square forms with additional string-based criteria. Each reach design is linked to a grading system that displays the potentially hazardous places based on the yield effect. The hotspot designs are saved in a pre-defined library, and the location interaction searches for hotspots using string matching. Although this method is precise, developing a range pattern requires a grid-based format foundation, which can be time consuming when the number of grids is large. By extracting basic topological features and showing them as design guidelines, Yu, Y. T. *et al.* [24] propose a DRC-based hotspot recognition. When in doubt, hotspot detection can be seen by looking at the process through a DRC engine. A matching-based hotspot characterization conspire is proposed in [27]. Data mining techniques are used to group the hotspots into groups. Each bunch's delegate hotspot is then identified and saved in a hotspot library for future hotspot identification. [27] relies on a distance metric of several example tests, which is defined as a weighted integral across the region where a couple of hotspot designs contrast (XOR of examples). It is sensitive to little variations or movements. For hotspot grouping, [28] proposes an Improved Tangent Space (ITS) based measurement. It is a supplement to the widely used tangent space algorithms [29–31] in the field of computer vision. The L2 standard of the distinction of the comparing turning elements of the polygons is the ITS measurement, which characterises a distance metric of a couple of polygons [29, 30]. The turning capacity of a polygon calculates the angle of the counter clockwise tangent as a component of the standardised circular length, which is calculated from a polygon's reference point. The ITS-based measurement is simple to register and is forgiving of minor form variations or movements. The hotspot setup can achieve improved precision using ITS-based measurement.

1.9 Improving Analysis Correlation

Examination miscorrelation exists when two unique devices return various outcomes for a similar investigation task (parasitic extraction, static timing analysis (STA), and so forth) even as they apply something very similar to "laws of physics" to similar information. As delineated in Figure 1.4, better precision generally comes at the expense of more calculation. Hence, miscorrelation between two examination reports is frequently the inescapable outcome of runtime effectiveness requirement. For instance, close down timing is excessively costly (device licenses, gradual examination speed, loops of timing window combination, query speed, number of corners, and so on) to be utilized inside close enhancement loop. Miscorrelation forces presentation of design protects groups as well as cynicism into the stream. For instance, if the place-and-route (P&R) instrument's STA report verifies that an endpoint has positive most terrible arrangement slack, while the signoff STA apparatus establishes that a similar endpoint has negative most obviously awful slack, a cycle (ECO fixing step) will be required. Then again, assuming the P&R instrument applies cynicism to guard band its miscorrelation to the sign off apparatus, this will cause unnecessary measuring, safeguarding or VT-swapping activities that cost region, power and design plan. Miscorrelation of timing examinations is especially unsafe: (i) timing conclusion can consume up to 60% of configuration time [32], and (ii) added guard bands do not just demolish power-speed-area compromises [33], but can likewise prompt non-convergence of the design signoff timer relationship. Relationship to signoff timing is the most significant objective for ML in back-end plan. Further developed correlations can give "better exactness for free" that moves the expense precision trade off (for example accomplishing the ML impact in Figure 1.4) and optimize iterations, completion time, overdesign, and instrument license uses along the whole way to definite design signoff. These models further develop precision of delay and slew assessments alongside by the timer correlation, with the end goal that less invocation of signoff STA are required during gradual gate sizing estimation [34]. [32] applies profound figuring out how to demonstrate and address difference between various STA apparatuses as for flip-flop setup time, cell arc delay, wire delay, stage deferral, and way slack at timing endpoints. The methodology accomplishes significant (various stage delays) decreases in miscorrelation. Both a one-time preparing strategy utilizing artificial and genuine circuit topologies, as well as a incremental training stream during production utilization, are portrayed (Figure 1.4). A mix of electrical, functional and topological boundaries are utilized to foresee the incremental progress times and arc/path delays because of SI impacts. From this and different works, a clear "easy decision" is to utilize

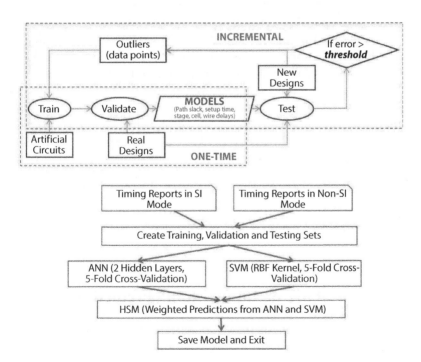

Figure 1.4 Flow and results for machine learning of static timing analysis tool miscorrelation [32–35].

Hybrid Surrogate Modelling (HSM) [32] to join anticipated values from various ML models into definite predictions. The profit from venture for new ML applications would be higher when x is bigger. Next Targets. [23] recognizes two close term augmentations in the domain of timer examination correlation. (1) PBA from GBA. Timing examination cynicism is decreased with path-based analysis (PBA), at the expense of essentially more prominent runtime than conventional graph-based analysis (GBA). In GBA, most exceedingly awful (resp. best) changes (for max (resp. min) delay analysis) are engendered at each pin along a timing path, prompting moderate appearance time estimates. PBA computes path explicit change and appearance times at each pin, decreasing cynicism that can comfortably surpass a phase delay. Figure 1.4 represents flow and results for machine learning of static timing analysis tool miscorrelation.

1.10   Role of ML in Data Path Placement

S. Ward *et al.* [12] suggested a programmed data path extraction in the accompanying new manner. Makes a decision about the various data path and afterward allots the positions to them to streamline it. This improvement is continued in an overall approach to driving or putting the data alongside new position stream as shown in Figure 1.5 [12]. SVM and ANN techniques are consolidated at the underlying training stage to segregate and pass judgment on the data path. When both procedures are used, the result is a competent model that is treated as a reduced model at run time. In the SVM model, a fault tolerance is determined by the arrangement of working data paths. In any event, ANN will generate choices from the training data, similar to how people organise their neurons. Whether it is a data path or a non-data path, accuracy of assessment is crucial. SVM and ANN are both capable of achieving this. Distinguishing data path design from opaque design is further improved, which can be addressed in the preparation stage of data learning models. To recognise the unique case, certain edge thresholds are set while involving SVM and AVM assessments.

1.11   Role of ML on Route Ability Prediction

The work [36–41] materials the main calculated study on route capacity forecast in light of Convolutional Neural Network. Subconsciously, that is clearly a promising course; however, it isn't all around concentrated beforehand. The method Route Net can just estimate general route ability

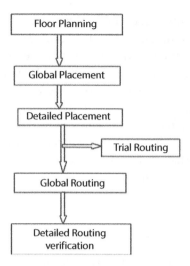

Figure 1.5 General physical design flow [36].

(Figure 1.5) in conditions of Design Rule Violation count thinking about macros [42]. Route Net accomplishes tantamount accuracy in contrast with that of worldwide routing; however, it is by and large significant degrees speedier really, assuming preparation period is regularly counted. Figure 1.5 shows general physical design flow to the best of our agreement; this is really the first route capacity predictor which incorporates both such extraordinary exactness and incredible speed. In anticipating DRC hotspot regions considering macros, it makes a huge improvement of half precision improvement versus worldwide routing. Moreover, Route Net remarkably outflanks SVM and calculated regression-centered expectation.

1.12 Conclusion

In this article, we have demonstrated the use of Artificial Intelligence in several aspects of the VLSI Logical and Physical Plan, such as assembly, miscorrelation, power inquiry, testing, mask synthesis, transition and connection delay, and CAD tools. However, AI has several applications in the VLSI design stages. Furthermore, the use of AI systems to VLSI backend design is still in its early stages. In the SRAF era, for example, pixel-by-pixel assumptions are necessary, and only direct models are utilised, limiting the usage of more complex models due to high computational costs. In general, OPC is only sensible to embrace direct models. Such advancement concerns necessitate the creation of a new cover image in a specific format. It deserves more investigation. It is unclear whether a generic representation of arrangement data exists or whether a customised integrate decision can be made. Furthermore, unlike domains with extensive AI assessment, such as image confirmation, where a large proportion of data is open, obtaining appropriate data in VLSI plan for planning powerful and exact models is often arduous and costly. As a result, it is critical to develop approaches to enhance showing precision while reducing the need for massive data so that AI may be widely adopted. These issues will be further looked into in the future.

References

1. Miller, A. (1989). From Expert Assistant to Design Verification: Applications of AI to VLSI Design, *Session 11Al, IEEE*, 2 (406–410).
2. Steinberg, L. I., & Mitchell, T. M. (1984). A knowledge based approach to VLSI CAD the redesign system. In *Proceedings of the 21st Design Automation Conference* (412–418). IEEE Publications.
3. Kowalski, T. J., & Thomas, D. E. (1983). The VLSI design automation assistant prototype system. In *20th Design Automation Conference* (479–483). IEEE Publications.
4. Kelly, Van E. (1984). The CRITTER system: Automated critiquing of digital circuit designs. In *Proceedings of the 21st Design Automation Conference* (419–425). IEEE Publications.
5. Steele, R. L. (1987). An expert system application in semicustom VLSI design. In A. O'Neill & D. Thomas (Eds.). *Proceedings of the 24th ACM/IEEE Design Automation Conference*, Acad. med. (679–688).
6. Farahat, H., Eldessouki, A., Mahmoud, M. Y., & Elsimary, H. (1989). An expert system for VLSI layout design, *International Conference on Systems Engineering* (529–532). IEEE Publications.
7. Stefik, M., & Conway, L. (1982). Towards the principled engineering of knowledge. *AI Magazine*, 3(3), 4–16. (Reprinted in *Readings from the AI Magazine*, Volumes 1-5, 1980-1985, 135-147, 1988).
8. Kim, J., & McDermott, J. P. (1983). TALIB: An IC layout design assistant. In *Proceedings of the AAAI* (197–201).
9. Rabbat, G. (1988). VLSI and AI are getting closer. *IEEE Circuits and Devices Magazine*, 4(1), 15–18. https://doi.org/10.1109/101.926
10. Kowalski, T. J., Geiger, D. J., Wolf, W. H., & Fichtner, W. (1985). The VLSI design automation assistant: From algorithms to silicon. *IEEE Design and Test of Computers*, 2(4), 33–43. https://doi.org/10.1109/MDT.1985.294721
11. Engineers garage [Web]. http://www.engineersgarage.com/articles/vlsi-design-future, Retrieved September 30 2012.

12. S. Ward, D. Ding, and D. Z. Pan, Pade: A high-performance placer with automatic datapath extraction and evaluation through high dimensional data learning, in *DAC Design Automation Conference 2012*, pp. 756–761, 2012.
13. Mitchell, T. (1997). *Machine learning.* McGraw-Hill. ISBN 0-07-042807-7, OCLC 36417892.
14. Koza, J. R., Bennett, F. H., Andre, D., & Keane, M. A. (1996). Automated design of both the topology and sizing of analog electrical circuits using genetic programming. *Artificial intelligence in design* 1996. Springer, Dordrecht. 151–170. https://doi.org/10.1007/978-94-009-0279-4_9
15. Hu, J., Niu, H., Carrasco, J., Lennox, B., & Arvin, F. (2020). Voronoi-based multi-robot autonomous exploration in unknown environments via deep reinforcement learning. *IEEE Transactions on Vehicular Technology*, 69(12), 14413–14423. https://doi.org/10.1109/TVT.2020.3034800
16. Bishop, C. M. (2006). *Pattern recognition and machine learning*, Springer, ISBN 978-0-387-31073-2.
17. Friedman, J. H. (1998). Data Mining and Statistics: What's the Connection? *Computing Science and Statistics*, 29(1), 3–9.
18. Zhou, V. (2019/12/20). Machine learning for beginners: An introduction to neural networks. Medium. Retrieved 2021/8/15.
19. Lin, Y., Xu, X., Ou, J., & Pan, D. Z. (2017). Machine learning for mask/wafer hotspot detection and mask synthesis. In *Photomask Technology*, 10451 p. 104510A. International Society for Optics and Photonics.
20. Matsunawa, T., Yu, B., & Pan, D. Z. (2016). Optical proximity correction with hierarchical bayes model. *Journal of Micro/Nanolithography, MEMS, and MOEMS*, 15(2), 009–021. https://doi.org/10.1117/1.JMM.15.2.021009
21. Chan, & Tuck-Boon, A. B. Kahng, Jiajia Li, and Siddhartha Nath. (2013). Optimization of overdrive signoff. In *18th Asia and South Pacific Design Automation Conference (ASP-DAC)* (344–349). IEEE Publications.
22. Duo Ding, D., Torres, J. A., & Pan, D. Z. (2011). High performance lithography hotspot detection with successively refined pattern identifications and machine learning. *IEEE Transactions on Computer-Aided Design of Integrated Circuits and Systems*, 30(11), 1621–1634. https://doi.org/10.1109/TCAD.2011.2164537
23. Wuu, J.-Y., Pikus, E. G., Torres, A., & Marek-Sadowska, M. (2011). Rapid layout pattern classification. In *IEEElACM Asia and South Pacific Design Automation Coriference (ASPDAC)*, 781–786.
24. Yu, Y. T., Lin, G.-H., Jiang, H.R. and Chiang, E. (2013). Machine-learning based hotspot detection using topological classification and critical feature extraction, in *IEEEIACM Design Automation Coriference (DAC)*, 671–676.
25. Xiao, Z., Du, Y., Tian, H., Wong, M. D., Yi, H., Wong, H.-S. P., & Zhang, H. (2014). Directed self-assembly (DSA) template pattern verification. In *IEEE/ACM Design Automation Conference (DAC)* (1–6).

26. Gao, J.-R., Yu, B., & Pan, D. Z. (2014). Accurate lithography hotspot detection based on PCA-SVM classifier with hierarchical data clustering. In *Proceedings of the SPIE*, 9053.
27. Yu, B., -Gao, R., Ding, D., Zeng, X., & Pan, D. Z. Accurate lithography hotspot detection based on principal component analysis-support vector machine classifier with hierarchical data clustering. *Journal of Micro Nanolithography, MEMS, and MOEMS* (1M3), 14(1), p. 011003, 2015.
28. Guo, J., Yang, E., Sinha, S., Chiang, C., & Zeng, X. (2012). Improved tangent space based distance metric for accurate lithographic hotspot classification. In *IEEE/ACM Design Automation Conference (DAC)* (1173–1178).
29. Arkin, E. M., Chew, L. P., Huttenlocher, D. P., Kedem, K., & Mitchell, J. S. B. (1991). An efficiently computable metric for comparing polygonal shapes. *IEEE Transactions on Pattern Analysis and Machine Intelligence*, 13(3), 209–216. https://doi.org/10.1109/34.75509
30. Latecki, L. J., & Lakamper, R. (2000). Shape similarity measure based on correspondence of visual parts. *IEEE Transactions on Pattern Analysis and Machine Intelligence*, 10, 1–6.
31. Lin, S.-Y., Chen, J.-Y., Li, J.-C., -Wen, Y., & Chang, S.-E. (2013). A novel fuzzy matching model for lithography hotspot detection. In *IEEE/ACM Design Automation Coriference (DAC)*, 681–686.
32. Han, S. S., Kahng, A. B., Nath, S., & Vydyanathan, A. (2014). A deep learning methodology to proliferate golden signoff timing. *Proceedings of the DATE*, p. 260:1-260:6.
33. Kahng, A. B., Lin, B., & Nath, S. (2013). Enhanced metamodeling techniques for high-dimensional IC design estimation problems. *Proceedings of the DATE* (1861–1866).
34.. Kahng, A. B., Lin, B., & Nath, S. (2013). High-dimensional metamodeling for prediction of clock tree synthesis outcomes. *Proceedings of the SLIP* (1–7).
35. Kahng, A. B., Luo, M., & Nath, S. (2015). SI for free: Machine learning of interconnect coupling delay and transition effects. *Proceedings of the SLIP* (1–8).
36. Xie, Zhiyao, Huang, Y.-H., Fang, G.Q., Ren, H., Fang, S.Y., Chen, Yiran, & Hu, J. (2018). RouteNet: Routability prediction for mixed-size designs using convolutional neural network. In *IEEE/ACM International Conference on Computer-Aided Design (ICCAD)* (1–8).
37. Farahat, H., Eldessouki, A., Mahmoud, M. Y. & Elsimary, H. (1989). An Expert System for VLSI Layout Design, *International Conference on Systems Engineering, IEEE*, 529-532.
38. Stefik, M., & Conway, L. (1988). Towards the Principled Engineering of Knowledge", *AI Magazine*, 3(3), 4-16, 1982. (Reprinted in *Readings from the AI Magazine*, 1-5, 1980-1985, 135-147, 1988.)
39. Kim, J., & McDermott, J.P. (1983). TALIB: An IC Layout Design Assistant, *In Proc. AAAI*, 197-201.

40. Rabbat, G. (1988). VLSI and AI are getting closer, *Circuits and Devices Magazine, IEEE*, 4 (1), 15-18.
41. Kowalski, T.J., Geiger, D. J., Wolf, W.H. & Fichtner, W. (1985). The VLSI Design Automation Assistant: From Algorithms to Silicon, *Design & Test of Computers, IEEE*, 2 (4), 33-43.
42. Tripathi, S.L., Saxena, S., & Mohapatra, S.K. (Eds.). (2020). *Advanced VLSI Design and Testability Issues* (1st ed.). CRC Press, Boca Raton. https://doi.org/10.1201/9781003083436

2

Design of an Accelerated Squarer Architecture Based on Yavadunam Sutra for Machine Learning

A.V. Ananthalakshmi*, P. Divyaparameswari and P. Kanimozhi

Department of ECE, Puducherry Technological University, Puducherry, India

Abstract

A novel acceleration strategy of a squarer architecture is proposed for machine learning so as to reduce the hardware complexity and thereby achieve superior performance. Complex mathematical operation can be greatly simplified by adopting Vedic mathematics. Efficient arithmetic operations are required to carry out real-time applications. Multipliers are frequently employed in signal processing. Hence multipliers can be designed using a squarer unit. Squaring Circuit offers a very good performance in terms of speed. Thus squaring module becomes the fundamental operation in any arithmetic unit. The squaring operation is frequently employed in cryptography also. On the whole, squaring operation is widely encountered in multipliers. While designing multipliers, it is essential to reduce the hardware complexity with less power consumption. Vedic mathematics simplifies the design concepts and thus paves the way for high-speed applications. On comparing the various Vedic sutras, Yavadunam sutra is highly efficient from logic utilization and is found to be suitable for high-speed digital applications. Hence, a squaring architecture has been designed using Yavadunam sutra, an ancient sutra of Vedic mathematics without using a multiplier circuit. The proposed acceleration strategy employs only addition operations. The design is simulated and realized using Xilinx Isim Simulator.

Keywords: Squarer circuit, Vedic multiplier, Yavadunam sutra

Corresponding author: anantha_av@ptuniv.edu.in

Abhishek Kumar, Suman Lata Tripathi, and K. Srinivasa Rao (eds.) Machine Learning for VLSI Chip Design, (19–32) © 2023 Scrivener Publishing LLC

2.1   Introduction

Recently, deep learning algorithms gained popularity in contrast to the classical method. In mobile and edge devices, for classifying Histogram of Oriented Gradients (HOG) feature extractor is mainly used in Support Vector Machine (SVM) classifier, so as to achieve remarkable performance and thereby try to bring down the hardware complexity. One should achieve this by reducing the computational complexity without compromising on accuracy. Area and power reduction plays a crucial role in VLSI system design. High-speed adders and multipliers are essential in the design of a high-performance system. To meet the demand in high-speed applications, the design of high-speed multipliers increases the hardware complexity as well as the power consumption. To overcome the above said drawback, Vedic mathematics finds its extensive use in the design of hardware arithmetic units. Thus this work employs Vedic mathematics in the design of a squarer so as to achieve superior performance with reduced complexity.

The essential idea behind the Histogram of Object oriented Gradients Descriptor (HOD) is that the object appearance and shape of an image is identified using the intensity of gradient and edge direction. The gradient is computed using the following expression:

$$g = \sqrt{g_x^2 + g_y^2} \qquad (2.1)$$

In order to compute the gradient, squaring operation is required. This work focuses on the implementation of high-performance squarer architecture by reducing the complexity without compromising on accuracy.

Several works were reported in the literature on the design of a squarer architecture. Vedic mathematics uses simple techniques and hence can be applied in the implementation of any mathematical operation [1]. An n-bit squarer using Vedic multipliers was proposed in [2] in which generation of partial products and its summation were done simultaneously to speed up the process. However, this has increased the hardware complexity. High-speed binary squaring architecture was proposed in [3, 4] which was based on Urdhva Tiryagbhyam Sutra (UTS) technique. This work also offers good performance at the cost of logic density. The squarer circuit based on peasant multiplication technique was introduced in [5] but this design has also increased the area. Vedic mathematics is applied in the design of a binary squarer and cube architecture so as to minimize the power dissipation [6]. Yavadunam algorithm finds its use in the squarer architecture as it produces good performance [7]. Nikhilam Sutra rules [8] were employed in the design of a squaring unit. This architecture has improved the speed but at the cost of area. An 8-bit and a 16-bit squarer circuit was proposed in [9] based on Antyayordashakepi Sutra and duplex technique. Both the designs offered good performance but at the cost of logic density. In [10] an efficient squarer was proposed based on Yavadunam algorithm for high-speed digital applications. All previously reported works had designed a 2-bit squaring circuits using which higher order bit multipliers were designed [11, 12]. In any hardware implementation, delay, area and power consumption becomes the primary concern. High-speed arithmetic systems heavily depend on high-speed adders and multipliers which in turn depend on squarer circuits [13–15]. [16–18] presents the high-speed multiplier architectures. From the literature survey it is inferred that an n-bit squaring circuit based on a Vedic multiplier requires more logic gates and thus results in more area. As Yavadunam sutra is highly efficient for high-speed digital applications, this work focuses on the design of a 4-bit squarer using a 3-bit squarer by employing Yavadunam sutra [19]. Design of an accelerated HOD/SVM for object recognition is proposed in [20] by reducing the computational operations just by using the addition operation. Hardware accelerator for machine learning was proposed in [21] with an aim to reduce the computational complexity. A power efficient hardware accelerator using FPGA was proposed in [22]. The hardware implementation of UCB algorithm was proposed in [23].

2.2   Methods and Methodology

Though Yavadunam sutra has been considered as the powerful squaring algorithms there is no efficient hardware architecture. Thus to begin with, an n-bit squaring circuit using Yavadunam sutra is designed where n = 4. However, it has resulted in more logic utilization. Hence a n-bit squaring circuit is designed using an (n-1)-bit squaring circuit so as to achieve higher speed. However, the design of an n-bit squaring circuit based on (n-1)-bit squaring circuit not only achieves higher speed but has also consumed less gates than an n-bit multiplier and thus resulted in less logic area. The objective of this work is to design an n-bit squarer using an (n-1)-bit squarer and thereby to reduce the i. The main goal is to implement a squaring circuit that does not rely on an area-consuming multiplier.

2.2.1 Design of an n-Bit Squaring Circuit Based on (n-1)-Bit Squaring Circuit Architecture

In the design of an n-bit squaring circuit based on (n-1)-bit squaring circuit where 'n' = 4, the numbers from 0 to 15 are considered. By keeping 8[1000] as the centre value, the numbers are divided into three cases as shown in Figure 2.1. The numbers below 8[1000] are treated as a single case, A < B. The numbers greater than 8[1000] are considered as the second case, i.e., A > B. In the third case, the centre value A = B is taken into account.

From Figure 2.1,
A ➔ Four bit input,
B ➔ Base (deficiency) of input, i.e., base value B = 1000 since the input is a 4-bit data.

2.2.1.1 Architecture for Case 1: A < B

Figure 2.2 shows the block diagram of an n-bit squaring circuit based on (n-1)-bit squaring circuit for case 1, i.e., A < B where 'n' = 4. A 4-bit input that must be squared meets the condition of being less than 8[1000]. 'D' represents A[(n-2) down to zero] where 'n' = 4. As a result, 4 – 2 = 2, and we must consider from 0th to 2nd bit of the input. The value of 'D' is sent to the 3-bit squaring circuit, which performs squaring operations and outputs as 6-bit labeled 'M'. As we are squaring 4-bit numbers, we need 8-bit output, so two zeros are placed before the value of 'M' and labeled as 'X', where 'X' is the squared output of 'A'.

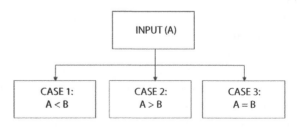

Figure 2.1 Block diagram for n-bit squaring circuit based on (n-1)-bit squaring circuit.

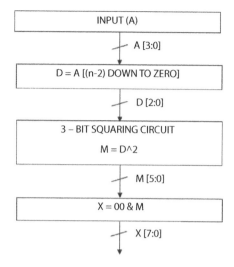

Figure 2.2 Block diagram for n-bit squaring circuit based on (n-1)-bit squaring circuit for case 1: a < b.

2.2.1.1.1   (n-1) – Bit Squaring Architecture

(n-1)-bit squaring circuit is used in the design of an n-bit squarer circuit where 'n' = 4. Table 2.1 presents the truth table for (n-1)-bit squaring circuit. The (n-1)-bit squaring circuit has been designed only using the basic logic gates as represented in Figure 2.3.

Table 2.1 Truth table for (n-1) – bit squaring circuit.

N(3)	N(2)	N(1)	S(6)	S(5)	S(4)	S(3)	S(2)	S(1)
0	0	0	0	0	0	0	0	0
0	0	1	0	0	0	0	0	1
0	1	0	0	0	0	1	0	0
0	1	1	0	0	1	0	0	1
1	0	0	0	1	0	0	0	0
1	0	1	0	1	1	0	0	1
1	1	0	1	0	0	1	0	0
1	1	1	1	1	0	0	0	1

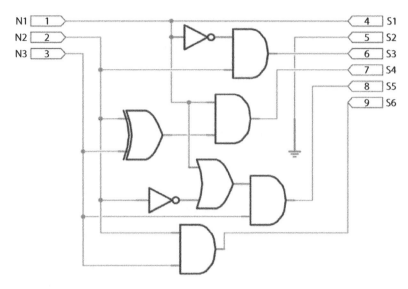

Figure 2.3 Architecture for 3 – bit squaring circuit.

2.2.1.2 *Architecture for Case 2: A > B*

Figure 2.4 presents the block diagram for n-bit squaring circuit based on (n-1)-bit squaring circuit for case 2 where A > B with the assumption 'n' = 4. The input block receives the 4-bit number that we want to square. The input (A) is sent to a block called 2's complement, which inverts the 4-bit input and then adds one, yielding 'E' as the output. As the input to the A < B block meets the first case's criteria, the steps taken in case 1 are repeated here, and the result is labeled as 'M'. The input 'A' is left shifted 4 times since 'n' = 4. As a result, the input is shifted left by four times, and the output is labeled as 'I'. One of two 8-bit ripple carry adder is used to combine the 'M' and 'I' outputs, which are labeled as 'H'. Another is used to combine the 'H' and 'I' outputs into a single 'Z' output. To obtain an 8-bit output, the first eight bits of 'Z' are treated as the squared output of a 4-bit input (A).

Thus if A > B, then the squarer operation is implemented using adder, subtractor and shift elements alone.

2.2.1.3 *Architecture for Case 3: A = B*

Figure 2.5 presents the block diagram for n-bit squaring circuit based on (n-1)-bit squaring circuit case 3, i.e., A = B. In this case, the centre value 8[1000] is used to calculate the squared output of 8 as 64. Simply shift the input, i.e., 8[1000], left three times to obtain the required output.

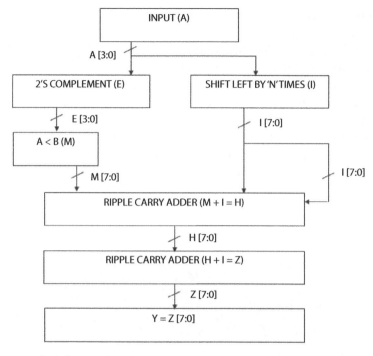

Figure 2.4 Block diagram for n-bit squaring circuit based on (n-1)-bit squaring circuit for a > b.

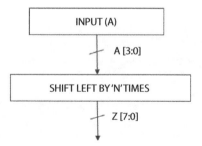

Figure 2.5 Block diagram for n-bit squaring circuit based on (n-1)-bit squaring circuit for a = b.

In Figure 2.5, if A = B, then the squarer operation is implemented using left shift operation.

2.3   Results and Discussion

In a 4-bit squaring circuit based on Vedic multiplier, a 2-bit multiplier is required which consists of a half adder whose simulated output is illustrated as shown in Figure 2.6. The binary inputs are 1 and 0 and the outputs are 1 and 0, respectively.

The full adder functionality is shown in Figure 2.7. The inputs are 1, 1, 0 and the outputs are 0 and 1 respectively.

The functional verification of a 4-bit ripple carry adder is shown in Figure 2.8. The inputs are 0001, 0000 and 1 and the 4-bit sum is 0010 and carry is 0.

The functional verification of a 2-bit multiplier is shown in Figure 2.9 where 'a' and 'b' are inputs and produces output as 'p'. The values of input 'a' and 'b' are 2 and 3 and produces output 'p' as 6, respectively.

Figure 2.6 Half adder output.

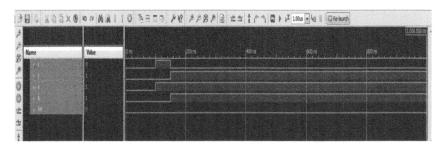

Figure 2.7 Full adder output.

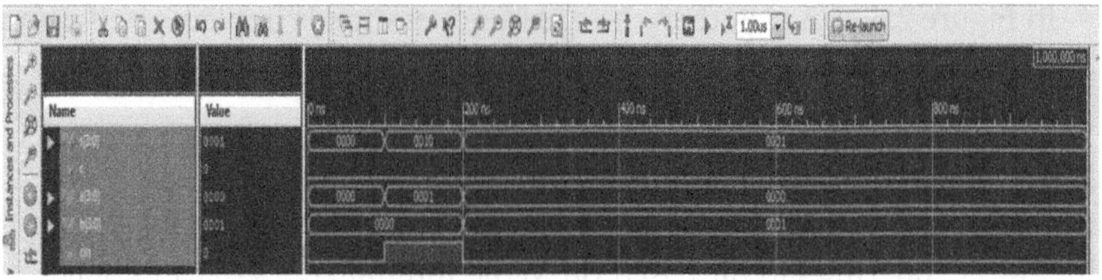

Figure 2.8 4-bit ripple carry adder output.

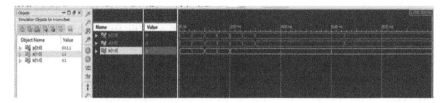

Figure 2.9 2-bit multiplier output.

A 4-bit multiplier is needed in a 4-bit squaring circuit based on Vedic multiplier, whose output is shown below in Figure 2.10. The inputs to 4-bit multiplier are 'a' and 'b' and produces 'p' as output. The inputs 'a' and 'b' are 5 and 5 and produce the value of 'p' as 25, respectively.

The output of an n-bit squaring circuit where 'n' = 4 based on Vedic multiplier is shown in Figure 2.11. The input is 15 and the squared output is 225.

The simulation result of an (n-1)-bit squaring circuit where 'n' = 4 is shown in Figure 2.12. The input is 3 and the squared output is 9.

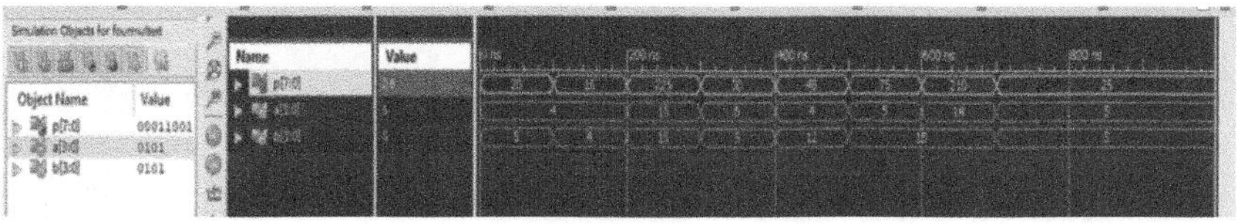

Figure 2.10 4-bit Vedic multiplier output.

Figure 2.11 n-bit squaring circuit based on Vedic multiplier output where 'n' = 4.

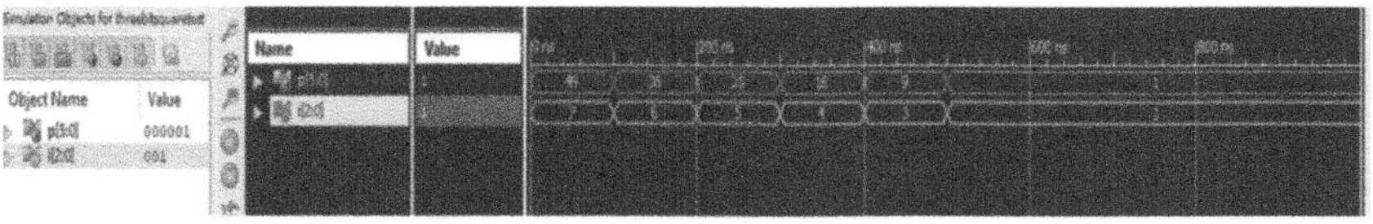

Figure 2.12 (n-1)-bit squaring circuit output where 'n' = 3.

The simulation output of an n-bit squaring circuit based on a (n-1)-bit squaring circuit is shown in Figure 2.13, where 'a' is the input to be squared and 'p' is the squared output of 'a'. Figure 2.13 shows that the input value of 'a' is 15 and produces 225 as the squared output of 'a' respectively.

Table 2.2 presents a comparison between an n-bit squaring circuit based on Vedic multiplier and an n-bit squaring circuit based on (n-1)-bit squaring circuit, where delay, area and logic utilization are compared. The logic utilization of an n-bit squaring circuit based on an (n-1)-bit squaring circuit is reduced by 18% where as the delay is retained.

Table 2.3 compares the number of gates used in an n-bit squaring circuit based on Vedic multiplier and an n-bit squaring circuit based on a (n-1)-bit squaring circuit. From the results, it is inferred that logic complexity of the latter is approximately half of that in the former.

As the number of transistors used determines the size of an integrated circuit, the number of transistors required in an n-bit squaring circuit based on Vedic mathematics will be definitely more when compared to an n-bit squaring circuit based on an (n-1)-bit squaring circuit as the logic gates required is more in the former when compared to the latter.

Figure 2.13 n-bit squaring circuit based on (n-1)-bit squaring circuit output where 'n' = 4.

Table 2.2 Comparison between squaring circuit based on Vedic multiplier and squaring circuit based on 3-bit squaring circuit.

Performance parameters	Squaring circuit based on Vedic multiplier	Squaring circuit based on 3-bit squaring circuit
Power	0.019W	0.018W
Delay	5.537ns	5.537ns
Logic Utilization	9 (56%)	6 (38%)

Table 2.3 Logic utilization for squaring circuit based on Vedic multiplier and squaring circuit based on 3-bit squaring circuit.

Logic utilization	Squaring circuit based on Vedic multiplier	Squaring circuit based on 3-bit squaring circuit
4 – Bit RCA	3	-
8 – Bit RCA	1	2
Full Adder	30	16
Half Adder	4	-
Full Subractor	1	-
And Gate	80	36
Or Gate	29	17
XOR Gate	64	33
Not Gate	16	2
2 Bit Multiplier	4	-
3 Bit Squaring Circuit	-	1

2.4   Conclusion

The performance of any VLSI implementation heavily depends on power, area and speed. For more accuracy and to simplify the hardware implementation one can apply Vedic mathematics. The n-bit squaring circuit based on Vedic multiplier has the disadvantage of requiring more logic gates and thus occupying more space with a greater number of logic elements. The n-bit squaring circuit design, which is based on a (n-1)-bit squaring circuit has fewer logic gates, takes up less space, and employs fewer transistors, resulting in the reduction in the size of the integrated circuit. When compared to a multiplier-based squaring circuit, this results in a 66% reduction in logic utilization, thus reducing the hardware complexity.

References

1. Fatemah K, Al-Assfor.; Israa S, Al-Furati.; Abdulmuttalib T, Rashid.; Vedic-Based Squarers with High Performance. *Indonesian Journal of Electrical Engineering and Informatics (IJEEI)* **2021**, 9, 1, 163-172.
2. Kasliwal P. S.; Patil, P; Gautam D, K.; Performance evaluation of squaring operation by vedic mathematics. *IETE Journal of Research* **2011**, 57, 1, 39–41.
3. Sethi, K.; Panda, R.; An improved squaring circuit for binary numbers. *International Journal of Advanced Computer Science and Applications* **2012**, 3, 2, 111–116.
4. Kumar, A.; Kumar, D.; Hardware implementation of 16 * 16 bit multiplier and square using Vedic mathematics. *International Conference on Signal, Image and Video Processing (ICSIVP)* **2012**, 309-314.
5. Kumar G. G.; Sudhakar C. V.; Babu M.N.; Design of high speed Vedic square by using Vedic multiplication techniques. *International Journal of Scientific & Engineering Research* **2013**, 4, 1, 1–4.
6. Ramanammma, P.; Low power square and cube architectures using Vedic Sutras. *International Journal of Engineering Research and General Science* **2017**, 5, 3, 241–248.
7. Deepa, A.; Marimuthu C, N.; High speed VLSI architecture for squaring binary numbers using Yavadunam Sutra and bit reduction technique. *International Journal of Applied Engineering Research* **2018**, 13, 6, 4471–4474.
8. Nithyashree, S.; Chandu, Y.; Design of an efficient vedic binary squaring circuit. *3rd IEEE International Conference on Recent Trends in Electronics, Information and Communication Technology, RTEICT 2018 - Proceedings*, **2018**, 362–366.
9. Barve, S.; Raveendran, S.; Korde, C.; Panigrahi, T.; Nithin Kumar Y, B.; Vasantha M, H.; FPGA implementation of square and cube architecture using vedic mathematics. *Proceedings - 2018 IEEE 4th International Symposium on Smart Electronic Systems, ISES*, **2018**, 6–10.
10. Deepa, A.; Marimuthu C, N.; VLSI Design of a Squaring Architecture Based on Yavadunam Sutra of Vedic Mathematics. *Proceedings of the International Conference on Electronics and Sustainable Communication Systems (ICESC)* **2020**, 1162–1167.
11. Akhter, S.; Chaturvedi, S.; Khan, S.; A distinctive approach for vedic-based squaring circuit. *International Conference on Signal Process. Integrated Networks, Spain* **2020**, 2, 27–30.
12. Koyada, B.; Meghana, N.; Jaleel M. O.; Jeripotula P. R.; A comparative study on adders. *Proceedings of the 2017 International Conference on Wireless Communications, Signal Processing and Networking, WiSPNET*, **2018**, 2206–2230.
13. Kandula B. S.; Kalluru P. V.; Inty S, P.; Design of area efficient VLSI architecture for carry select adder using logic optimization technique. *Computational Intelligence* **2020**, 1–11.

14. Kumar N. U.; Sindhuri K. B.; Teja K. D.; Satish D. S.; Implementation and comparison of VLSI architectures of 16-bit carry select adder using Brent Kung adder. *Innovations in Power and Advanced Computing Technologies, I-PACT,* **2017**, 1–7.

15. Yaswanth, D.; Nagaraj, S.; Vijeth R. V.; Design and analysis of high speed and low area vedic multiplier using carry select adder. *International Conference on Emerging Trends in Information Technology and Engineering, ICETITE,* **2020**, 8–12.

16. Deepa, A.; Marimuthu C. N.; VLSI Design of a Squaring Architecture Based on Yavadunam Sutra of Vedic Mathematics. *International Conference on Electronics and Sustainable Communications Systems,* **2020**.

17. Deepa, A; Marimuthu C. N.; Murugesan; An Efficient High Speed Squaring and Multiplier Architecture using Yavadunam Sutra and Bit Reduction Technique. *Journal of Physics Conference Series,* **2020**, 1432, 012080.

18. Deepa, A.; Marimuthu C. N.; Design of high speed Vedic Square and Multiplier Architecture Using Yavadunam Sutra. *Sadhana Indian Academy of Sciences,* **2019**, 44, 9, 97, 1-10.

19. Deepa, A.; Marimuthu C. N.; High Speed VLSI Architecture for Squaring Binary Numbers Using Yavadunam Sutra and Bit Reduction Technique. *International Journal of Applied Engineering Research,* **2018**, 13, 6, 4471- 4474.

20. Shi, Lilong; Wang, Chunji; Wang, Yibing; Oh Kim, Kwang; Accelerated HOG + SVM for Object Recognition. *Electronic Imaging Intelligent Robotics and Industrial Applications using Computer Vision,* **2021**, 317-1-317-3, **DOI:** https://doi.org/10.2352/ISSN.2470-1173.2021.6.IRIACV-317.

21. Li, Du; Yuan, Du; Hardware Accelerator for Machine Learning. *Machine Learning* **2017**, DOI: 10.5772/intechopen.72845.

22. JiUn, Hong; Saad, Arslan; TaeGeon, Lee; HyungWon, Kim; Design of power - efficient training accelerator for convolution neural networks, *Electronics,* **2017**, 10, 7, 787, https://doi.org/10.3390/electronics10070787.

23. Nevena, Radovic; Milena, Zogovic; Hardware Implementation of the Upper Confidence-bound Algorithm for Reinforcement Learning, *Computers and Electrical Engineering,* **2021**, 96.

3

Machine Learning–Based VLSI Test and Verification

Jyoti Kandpal

Dept. of Electronics and Communication Engineering, National Institute of Technology Arunachal Pradesh, Pradesh, India

Abstract

To test Integrated Chips, test pattern generation and fault simulation are vital. Testing verifies a circuit's accuracy regarding gates and connections between them. The fundamental purpose of testing is to model the circuit's various activities. Several Electronic Design Automation tools for fault identification and test pattern development are available to simulate circuits for structural testing. This chapter gives a brief idea of machine learning techniques: defect identification and test pattern generation at various abstraction levels.

Keywords: VLSI testing, Electronic Design Automation (EDA), machine learning

3.1 Introduction

With the emergence of complementary metal-oxide-semiconductor (CMOS) technology, a new circuit design paradigm with low power consumption emerged. CMOS design techniques are frequently used for digital circuits with particularly large-scale integration (VLSI). Today's IC chips have billions of transistors on a single die. In addition to design, testing for manufacturing flaws is an essential component in the production cycle of digital IC chips since it affects dependability, cost, and delivery time. Effective testing is also essential to determine the chip's yield and information on process variations. Various areas of fault modelling, detection, diagnosis, fault simulation, built-in self-test, and

Email: jayakandpal27@gmail.com

Abhishek Kumar, Suman Lata Tripathi, and K. Srinivasa Rao (eds.) *Machine Learning for VLSI Chip Design,* (33–50) © 2023 Scrivener Publishing LLC

design-for-testability (DFT) have been extensively researched over the last three decades, resulting in fast test generation and fault-diagnostic algorithms testable designs. Several industrial tools for testing have been developed over the years. However, with the increasing sophistication of IC chips, the obstacles in testing, especially in diagnosis, have grown [1].

VLSI testing is an integral part of any design because it allows you to determine if there are any defects in the circuit. The accuracy of the circuit can be established through testing. Verification is another approach to testing a circuit's behavior. The significant distinction between testing and verification is that testing considers a circuit, whilst verification considers the design. The distinction between testing and verification is seen in Table 3.1.

The verification process is divided into two parts:

1. Simulation-based verification
2. Formal approaches

VLSI testing covers the full range of testing methods and structures integrated into a system-on-chip (SOC) to ensure manufactured devices' quality during manufacturing tests. Test methods often comprise malfunction simulation and test generation to provide quality test patterns to each device. In addition, the test structures frequently use particular design for testability (DFT) techniques to test the digital logic sections of the device, such as scan design and built-in self-test (BIST). As the issue gets identified, the company's testing costs for the final product will be reduced. The "Rule of Ten" is commonly used in the VLSI testing sector. It claims that as

Table 3.1 Difference between testing and verification.

Testing	Verification
Verifies the correctness of a manufactured hardware.	In this process verifies the correctness of a circuit.
Testing is a two-step process: a) Test generation b) Test application	They were performed by simulation or hardware emulation or formal methods.
Test application performed on every manufactured device.	They executed one prior manufacturing.
Responsible for the quality of the device.	Responsible for quality of design.

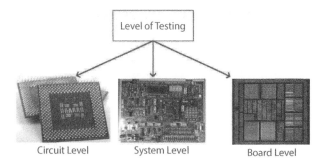

Figure 3.1 Stages of VLSI testing [1].

the testing phase progresses from one step to the next (Chip level > Board level > System-level > System-level at the field), the expense of identifying a flaw increases by a factor of ten. VLSI testing at various abstraction levels is depicted in Figure 3.1.

3.2   The VLSI Testing Process

There are two methods of the testing process.

3.2.1   Off-Chip Testing

The chip test equipment provides an external toolkit for this type of testing. Automated Test Equipment (ATE) is an example of Off-chip testing.

3.2.2   On-Chip Testing

In this method, test equipment is added on-chip and embedded resources to detect any flaw or defect in the circuit.

Equation 3.1 represents the testing formula that is followed in the industry [2]

$$Y = \frac{\text{Number of acceptable parts}}{\text{Total number of fabricated parts}} \qquad (3.1)$$

Y is the yield or the ratio of acceptance of the parts. In the initial phase, when the technology is new, the output is as low as 10%, but when the technology attains a certain level of maturity, it grows to a staggering 95%. Figure 3.2 represents VLSI testability and reliability.

VLSI TESTABILITY AND RELIABILITY

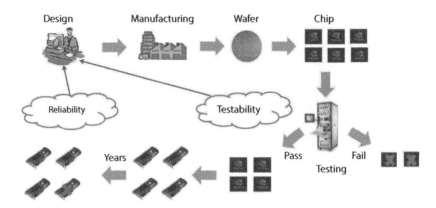

Figure 3.2 Example of VLSI testability and reliability [3].

In circuit-level testing is divided into two categories furthermore:

3.2.3   Combinational Circuit Testing

3.2.3.1   Fault Model

Fault Model (Stuck at model):

a. This method assumes selected wires (gate input or output) is stuck at logic 0 or 1.
b. It is a simplistic model and requires 2 n test input for n input circuit but for practical purposes in real life; it requires many test inputs.

3.2.3.2   Path Sensitizing

In this method, multi-wire testing is used in a circuit at the same time.

3.2.4   Sequential Circuit Testing

3.2.4.1   Scan Path Test

In this method, multiplexers are used to pass the FF inputs.

3.2.4.2   Built-In-Self Test (BIST)

In this method, a pseudorandom test vector is used in the feedback shift register.

3.2.4.3   Boundary Scan Test (BST)

In this tests interconnect (wire lines) on printed circuit boards or sub-blocks inside an integrated circuit. Boundary scan is also widely used as a debugging method to watch integrated circuit pin states, measure voltage, or analyze sub-blocks inside an integrated circuit.

3.2.5   The Advantages of VLSI Testing

a) The complex testing process can be eliminated for PCB testing to minimize human intervention.
b) It eases the job of the test engineer and increases the efficiency multifold.
c) Drastically reduces the time spent on complex testing.
d) The coverage for all types of faults is expanded heavily.

Compared to IC design capability, integrated circuit technology is rapidly advancing. The VLSI computation process is a time-consuming and complex operation. VLSI developers must monitor and implement technology growth as it occurs daily and on a periodic basis to improve their design tools. Machine learning (ML) enters the VLSI field with improved design methodology, features, and capabilities [3].

ML has several features and methods, but it still has significant limits in solving problems. Consequently, ML opens up plenty of possibilities for collaboration in VLSI and computer-based design. Furthermore, the knowledge gathered by ML is used to design and implement computer chips. As a result, it is regarded as the first ML application. In recent years, knowledge gained from ML introduction classes has been used to handle and routinely employ computer-based design tools.

Previously, most chips were developed manually, resulting in excessively huge size and slow performance. Furthermore, verifying such hand-crafted chips is a complex and time-consuming operation. Because of these complications, an automated tool was created. Furthermore, this automation tool has been upgraded to include new functionalities.

Chip designers introduce new design methods frequently, such as memory combing, novel techniques in computing tasks, etc., which must be controlled in the design process. Many manufacturers, like Synopsys, Mentor Graphics, and Cadence, offer computer-aided design (CAD) tools that can be considered machine learning applications for chip design. AI (Artificial Intelligence) and ML revolutionize every enterprise with extremely substantial inputs due to technology advancement. Machine learning has made many essential modifications in the VLSI sector.

So far, ML has assisted the VLSI sector by maximizing EDA tools, which helps reduce design time and manufacturing costs. Furthermore, machine learning in VLSI design aids EDA tools in finding an optimal solution in case of scenarios by forecasting chip flaws, which saves money during manufacturing [4].

3.3   Machine Learning's Advantages in VLSI Design

The benefits of ML in the VLSI field are as follows below.

3.3.1   Ease in the Verification Process

Machine learning in VLSI design and verification is critical as the amount of data created by complex devices continues to grow, ensuring smooth operation without compromising performance or cost. For RTL implementation, ML assists in formulating test cases and suggests better Design flows.

3.3.2   Time-Saving

Different regression methods are used in machine learning to reduce the complexity; therefore, verification time is reduced.

3.3.3   3Ps (Power, Performance, Price)

Cadence and Synopsys are two EDA systems that continually incorporate machine learning techniques to improve design stimulation and redesign the three Ps.

Figure 3.3 presents the machine learning model in the VLSI testing field.

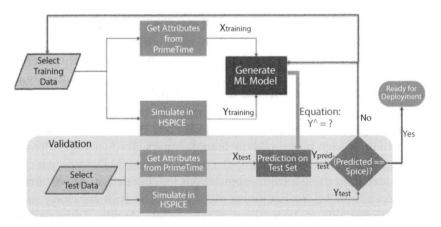

Figure 3.3 Machine learning model for testing [2].

3.4   Electronic Design Automation (EDA)

Electronic design automation (EDA) tools routinely are required to handle billions of entities at lower levels of abstraction. Furthermore, the number of components in a design increases with refinement and abstraction levels. Therefore, these tools need to operate on voluminous data and complex models to accomplish various tasks that can be categorized as follows.

a) **Estimate**: Typically, we need to make estimates based on incomplete information or designer-provided hints.

b) **Infer dependencies**: The given design data can be voluminous, and finding dependencies among various input parameters can be challenging.

c) **Transform**: We need to refine design information based on optimality criteria and constraints. It can also involve transforming a design's behavioural, structural, and physical views. The quality of results (QoR) in accomplishing the above tasks can often be improved by statistical data

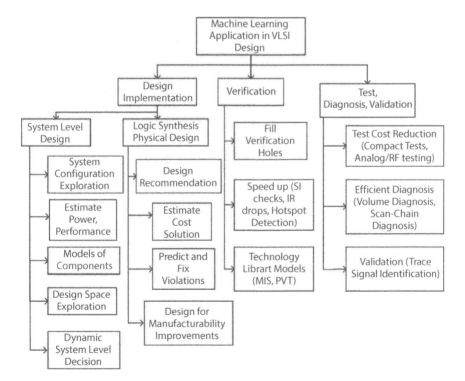

Figure 3.4 Applications of ML in VLSI design [1].

analysis, learning from examples, and encapsulating the designer's intelligence into an EDA tool.

There have been tremendous advancements in ML tools and technology in recent times. These advancements were facilitated by novel mathematical formulations and powerful computing resources that allow massive data processing. Consequently, a plethora of freely available tools to implement ML techniques and algorithms are available to us. Therefore, ML techniques are now widely employed in VLSI design. These techniques have improved the designer's productivity, tackled complex problems more efficiently, and provided alternative solutions. Figure 3.4 reports the ML application in the VLSI field.

VLSI design is a complex process. We decompose the design process into multiple steps, starting with system-level design and culminating in chip fabrication. We can apply ML and related techniques in design implementation, verification, testing, diagnosis, and validation stages. In this chapter, we discuss the applications of ML in the following steps:

a) System-Level Design
b) Logic Synthesis
c) Physical Design

3.4.1   System-Level Design

There are many challenges in designing state-of-the-art systems consisting of heterogeneous components such as GPUs, CPUs, and hardware accelerators. The difficulty arises due to the following reasons.

a) There is no complete implementation detail of many components at the system level. Therefore, we need to estimate the performance, power, and other attributes based on some abstract models. It is complex and error-prone.
b) We need to determine near-optimal system parameters for multiple objectives and constraints. Moreover, these constraints and objectives often depend on the application and change dynamically.
c) Due to an increase in the number and multitude of heterogeneous components, the design space or the solution space becomes big.
d) Traditional methods such as simulations are often too slow and expensive in exploring the design space for modern heterogeneous systems.

The abovementioned challenges are tackled by ML, which is discussed in the section below. Some of these challenges can be efficiently tackled by ML, as explained in the following section.

In designing a new system, we often need to choose a particular system configuration by estimating the system performance. For example, we need to select the CPU type, memory type, CPU frequency, memory size, bus type, and motherboard for a laptop. However, to make a choice, we need to predict the actual system performance. We can evaluate the system's performance by creating a predictive model based on neural networks and linear regression. These models can accurately determine system performance utilizing only a tiny portion of the design space and data from previously built systems.

We can also estimate heterogeneous systems' performance and power with more detail by applying ML techniques. In particular, we can measure these attributes with many test applications running on real hardware with various configurations. Furthermore, these measurements can train an ML model to produce the expected performance and power attributes for a system design parameter. After that, we can predict them for a new application running on various system configurations. Finally, we measure these values for a single structure and feed them to the ML model. Using these inputs, ML can quickly produce the estimate for various configurations with accuracy comparable to cycle-level simulators [5].

We also need to quickly estimate performance at the component level during design space exploration. For example, implementing hybrid memory architectures in scaled heterogeneous systems has advantages. We can combine nonvolatile memories (NVM) with the traditional DRAM to improve performance. To implement the hybrid memory architecture, we need to analyze the performance of various configurations. Traditionally, architectural-level memory simulators are used in these analyses. However, this approach suffers from long simulation time and inadequate design space exploration.

A better technique is to build an ML model that predicts various figures of merit for a memory. Then, we can train the ML model by a small set of simulated memory configurations. These predictive models can quickly report latency, bandwidth, power consumption, and other attributes for a given memory configuration.

In Sen and Imam [6], neural network, SVM, random forest (RF), and gradient boosting (GB) are tried for the ML model. It is reported that the SVM and RF methods yielded better accuracies compared with other models [6].

3.4.2 Logic Synthesis and Physical Design

Logic synthesis and physical design are the main tasks in the VLSI design flow. Due to computational complexity, we divide them into multiple steps. Some key steps are multi-level logic synthesis, budgeting, technology mapping, timing optimization, chip planning, placement, clock network synthesis, and routing. Nevertheless, each of these steps is still computationally difficult. Typically, EDA tools employ several heuristics to obtain a solution. Tool options and user-specified settings guide the heuristics. The QoR (Quality of Results) strongly depends on them. These steps are sequential. Therefore, the solution produced by a step impacts all subsequent tasks. A designer often adjusts the tool settings and inputs based on experience and intuition to achieve the desired QoR [7–10].

As explained in the following paragraphs, we can reduce design effort in these tasks and improve the QoR by employing ML tools and techniques.

One of the earliest attempts to reduce design effort using ML was Learning Apprentice for VLSI design (LEAP). LEAP acquires knowledge and learns rules by observing a designer and analyzing the problem-solving steps during their activities. Subsequently, it provides advice to the designer on design refinement and optimization. A designer can accept LEAP's advice or ignore it and manually carry out transformations. When a designer ignores the advice, LEAP considers it a training sample and updates its rule.

An ML-based tool for logic synthesis and physical design, such as a design advisor, needs to consider implementing the following tasks [11–14].

a) **Developing** a training set consists of data points with a design problem and its corresponding solution. For example, a data point can be an initial netlist, constraints, cost function, optimization settings, and the final netlist. We need to generate these data points for training or can acquire them from designers.

b) **Reduced representations of the training set:** The training data points typically contain many features. However, for efficient learning, we can reduce the dimensionality of the training set. For example, we can perform PCA and retain the most relevant input features.

c) **Learning to produce the optimum output:** The training data points that we collect from the existing EDA tools are, typically, not the mathematical optimum. On the other hand, these tools give the best possible solution that could be acceptable to the designers. Therefore, training data does not represent the ground truth of the problem. Moreover, data can be sparse and biased because some specific tools generate those results. We can employ statistical models such as Bayesian neural networks (BNNs) to tackle this problem. BNNs have weights and biases specified as distributions instead of scalar values. Therefore, it can tackle disturbances due to noisy or incomplete training sets.

d) **Dynamic updates:** We expect the ML-based design adviser to continue learning from the new design problems. We can use reinforcement learning to adjust the model dynamically.

3.4.3   Test, Diagnosis, and Validation

ML techniques also imply post-fabrication testing, diagnosis of failures, and validation of functionality. The ability of ML models to work efficiently on large data sets can be helpful in these applications [15, 16].

We can reduce the test cost by removing redundant tests. We can use ML to mine the test set and eliminate the redundant tests. We can consider a test redundant if we can predict its output using other tests that we are not removing. For example, we can use a statistical learning methodology based on decision trees to eliminate redundant tests. We should ensure maintaining product quality and limiting yield loss while removing difficulties.

We can also apply ML-based techniques to test analog/RF devices to reduce cost. However, it is challenging to maintain test errors in ML-based analog/RF device testing to an acceptable level. Therefore, we can adopt a two-tier test approach. For example, Stratigopoulos and Makris [17] developed a neural system-based framework that produces both the pass/fail labels and the confidence level in its prediction. If the confidence is low, traditional and more expensive specification testing is employed to reach a final decision. Thus, the cost advantage of ML-based analog/RF testing is leveraged. Note that the test quality is not sacrificed in the two-tier test approach [17]. We can employ a similar strategy for other verification problems where ML-induced errors are critical.

ML-based strategies are used to diagnose manufacturing defects. These methods provide alternatives to the traditional exploring of the causal relationship [18]. It can reduce the runtime complexity of the conventional diagnosis methods, especially for volume diagnosis. Wang and Wei [19] reported that defect locations are found for most defective chips even with highly compressed output responses.

Note that the scan chain patterns are insufficient to determine the failing flip-flop in a scan chain. Therefore, diagnosis methodologies need to identify defective scan cell(s) on a faulty scan chain. Unsupervised ML techniques based on the Bayes theorem are used to tolerate noises [20].

Another problem that can utilize the capabilities of ML is post-silicon validation. Before production, we carry out post-silicon validation to ensure that the silicon functions as expected under on-field operating conditions. For this purpose, we need to identify a small set of traceable signals for debugging and state restoration. Unfortunately, traditional techniques such as simulation take high runtime in identifying traceable signs. Alternatively, we can employ ML-based techniques for efficient signal selection. For example, we can train an ML with a few simulations runs. Subsequently, we can use this model to identify beneficial trace signals instead of employing time-consuming simulations [21].

3.5   Verification

We can employ techniques to improve and augment traditional verification methodologies in the following ways:

a) Traditional verification often makes certain assumptions to simplify its implementation. Consequently, it can leave some verification holes, or we sacrifice the QoR of a design. ML-based verifications can consider a larger verification domain. Thus, they can fill these holes and make validation more robust.

b) Traditional verification can take more runtime in finding patterns in a design. However, ML-based verification can search efficiently and produce results faster.

c) Traditional verification employs some abstract models for a circuit. ML can augment such models or replace them.

In the following section, we will discuss the application of ML in the Verification of VLSI chips. In simulation-based logic verification, we can use ML to quickly fill the coverage holes or reduce the runtime. Traditionally, we apply randomly generated test stimuli and observe their response. In addition, we often incorporate coverage-directed test generation (CDG) to improve coverage within a time limit. However, it is challenging to predict the constraints that can produce test stimuli with a high range.

ML techniques can generate the bias that directs CDG towards improved coverage. ML techniques are added to the feedback loop of CDG to produce new directives or preferences for obtaining stimuli that fill coverage holes. The ML model can also learn dynamically and screen stimuli before sending them for verification. For example, ANN can extract features of stimuli and select only critical ones for validation. Thus, we can filter out many stimuli and accelerate the overall verification process.

Some verification steps, such as signal integrity (SI) checks, take significant runtime. At advanced process nodes, SI effects are critical. It changes the delay and slew of signals due to the coupling capacitance and switching activity in the neighboring wires. We can employ ML techniques to estimate the SI effects quickly [22].

First, we identify Applications of ML in VLSI Design parameters on which SI effects depend. Some of the parameters that impact SI effects are: nominal (without considering SI) delay and slew, clock period, resistance, coupling capacitance, toggle rate, the logical effort of the driver, and temporal alignment of victim and aggressor signals. We can train an ML model such as ANN or SVM to predict SI-induced changes in delay and slew. Since ML models can capture dependency in a high-dimensional space, we can utilize them for easy verification. However, we should ensure that the errors produced by ML models are tolerable for our verification purpose.

Another approach to estimating SI effects is using anomaly detection (AD) techniques. AD techniques are popularly employed to detect anomalies in financial transactions. However, we can train an ML model, such as a contractive autoencoder (CA), with the features of SI-free time-domain waveforms. Subsequently, we use the trained model to identify anomalies due to SI effects. We can use both unsupervised and semi-supervised AD techniques [23].

We can employ ML techniques to efficiently fix IR drop problems in an integrated circuit [24]. Traditionally, we carry out dynamic IR drop analysis at the end of design flows. Then, any IR drop problem is corrected by Engineering Change Order (ECO) based on the designer's experience. Typically, we cannot identify and fix all the IR drop problems together. Consequently, we need to carry out dynamic IR drop analysis and ECO iteratively until we have corrected all the IR drop issues.

However, IR drop analysis takes significant runtime and the designer's effort. We can reduce the iterations in IR drop signoff by employing ML to predict all the potential IR drop issues and fix them together. Firstly, by ML-based clustering techniques, we identify high IR drop regions. Subsequently, small regional ML-based models are built on local features. Using these regional models, IR drop problems are identified and fixed.

After correcting all the violations, a dynamic IR drop check is finally done for signoff. If some violations still exist, we repeat the process till all the IR drop issues are corrected.

We can use ML techniques in physical verification for problems such as lithographic hotspot detection [25]. For example, we can efficiently detect lithographic hotspots by defining signatures of hotspots and a hierarchically refined detection flow consisting of ML kernels, ANN, and SVM. We can also employ a dictionary learning approach with an online learning model to extract features from the layout [26].

Another area where we can apply ML techniques is the technology library models. Technology libraries form the bedrock of digital VLSI design. Traditionally, timing and other attributes of normal cells are modelled in technology libraries as look-up tables. However, these attributes can be conveniently derived and compactly represented using ML techniques. Furthermore, the ML-models can efficiently exploit the intrinsic degrees of variation in the data.

Using ML techniques, Shashank Ram and Saurabh [27] discussed the effects of multi-input switching (MIS). Traditionally, we ignore MIS effects in timing analysis. Instead, we employ a delay model that assumes only a single input switching (SIS) for a gate during a transition. For SIS, the side inputs are held constant to non-controlling values. However, ignoring MIS effects can lead to overestimating or underestimating a gate delay. We have examined the impact of MIS on the delay of different types of gates under varying conditions. We can model the MIS-effect by deriving a corrective quantity called MIS-SIS difference (MSD). We obtain MIS delay by adding MSD to the conventional SIS delay under varying conditions.

There are several benefits of adopting ML-based techniques for modelling MIS effects. First, we can represent multi-dimensional data using a learning-based model compactly. It can capture the dependency of MIS effects on multiple input parameters and efficiently exploit them in compact representation. In contrast, traditional interpolation-based models have a large disk size and loading time, especially at advanced process nodes. Moreover, incorporating MIS effects in advanced delay models will require a drastic change in the delay calculator and is challenging. Therefore, we have modelled the MIS effect as an incremental corrective quantity over SIS delay. It fits easily with the existing design flows and delay calculators.

We have employed the ML-based MIS model to perform MIS-aware timing analysis. It involves reading MIS-aware timing libraries and reconstructing the original ANN. Since the ANNs are compact, the time consumed in the reconstruction of ANNs is insignificant. Subsequently, we compute the MSD for each relevant timing arc using the circuit conditions.

Using MSD, we adjust the SIS delay and generate the MIS-annotated timing reports. It is demonstrated that ML-based MIS modelling can improve the accuracy of timing analysis. For example, for some benchmark circuits, traditional SIS-based delay differs from the corresponding SPICE-computed delay by 120%. However, the ML-based model produces delays with less than 3% errors. The runtime overhead of MIS-aware timing analysis is also negligible. Shashank Ram and Saurabh [27] can be extended to create a single composite MIS model for different process voltage temperature (PVT) conditions. In the future, we expect that we can efficiently represent other complicated circuit and transistor-level empirical models using ML models.

3.6   Challenges

In the previous sections, we discussed various applications of ML techniques in VLSI design. Nevertheless, some challenges are involved in adopting ML techniques in conventional design flows. ML techniques' effectiveness in VLSI design depends on complex design data [33, 34]. Therefore, producing competitive results repeatedly on varying design data is challenging for many applications.

Moreover, training an ML model requires extracting voluminous data from a traditional or a detailed model. Sometimes it is challenging to generate such a training data set. Sometimes, these training data are far from the ground truth or contain many noises. Handling such a training set is challenging. ML-based design flows can disrupt the traditional design flows and be expensive to deploy.

Moreover, applying ML-based EDA tools may not produce expected results immediately. There is some non-determinism associated with ML-based applications. In the initial stages, there are not enough training data. Consequently, an ML-based EDA tool cannot guarantee accurate results. Therefore, adopting ML-based solutions in design flows is challenging for VLSI designers. Nevertheless, in the long run, ML-based techniques could deliver rich dividends.

3.7   Conclusion

ML offers efficient solutions for many VLSI design problems [28–32]. It is particularly suitable for complex problems for which we have readily available data to learn from and predict. With technological advancement, we expect that such design problems will increase. The advances in EDA tools will also help develop more efficient ML-specific hardware. The ML-specific hardware can accelerate the growth in ML technology. The advancement in ML technologies can further boost their applications in developing complex EDA tools. Thus, there is a synergic relationship between these two technologies. These technologies can benefit many other domains and applications in the long run.

References

1. Saini, S., Lata, K., & Sinha, G. R. (Eds.). (2021). *VLSI and Hardware Implementations Using Modern Machine Learning Methods*. CRC Press.
2. Rabaey, J. M., Chandrakasan, A. P., & Nikolic, B. (2002). *Digital integrated circuits* (Vol. 2). Englewood Cliffs: Prentice hall.
3. Ren M., & Mehta M. (2019). *Using machine learning for VLSI testability and reliability*. Nvidia.
4. Ozisikyilmaz, B., Memik, G., & Choudhary, A. (2008, June). Efficient system design space exploration using machine learning techniques. In *2008 45th ACM/IEEE Design Automation Conference* (pp. 966-969). IEEE.
5. Greathouse, J. L., & Loh, G. H. (2018, November). Machine learning for performance and power modelling of heterogeneous systems. In *2018 IEEE/ACM International Conference on Computer-Aided Design (ICCAD)* (pp. 1-6). IEEE.
6. Sen, S., & Imam, N. (2019, September). Machine learning based design space exploration for hybrid main-memory design. In *Proceedings of the International Symposium on Memory Systems* (pp. 480-489).
7. Zuluaga, M., Krause, A., Milder, P., & Püschel, M. (2012, June). "Smart" design space sampling to predict Pareto-optimal solutions. In *Proceedings of the 13th ACM SIGPLAN/SIGBED International Conference on Languages, Compilers, Tools and Theory for Embedded Systems* (pp. 119-128).
8. Liu, H. Y., & Carloni, L. P. (2013, May). On learning-based methods for design-space exploration with high-level synthesis. In *Proceedings of the 50th Annual Design Automation Conference* (pp. 1-7).
9. Mahapatra, A., & Schafer, B. C. (2014, May). Machine-learning based simulated annealer method for high level synthesis design space exploration. In *Proceedings of the 2014 Electronic System Level Synthesis Conference (ESLsyn)* (pp. 1-6). IEEE.
10. Kim, R. G., Doppa, J. R., & Pande, P. P. (2018, November). Machine learning for design space exploration and optimization of manycore systems. In *2018 IEEE/ACM International Conference on Computer-Aided Design (ICCAD)* (pp. 1-6). IEEE.

11. Pagani, S., Manoj, P. S., Jantsch, A., & Henkel, J. (2018). Machine learning for power, energy, and thermal management on multicore processors: A survey. *IEEE Transactions on Computer-Aided Design of Integrated Circuits and Systems, 39*(1), 101-116.

12. Xiao, Y., Nazarian, S., & Bogdan, P. (2019). Self-optimizing and self-programming computing systems: A combined compiler, complex networks, and machine learning approach. *IEEE Transactions on Very Large Scale Integration (VLSI) Systems, 27*(6), 1416-1427.

13. Mitchell, T. M., Mabadevan, S., & Steinberg, L. I. (1990). LEAP: A learning apprentice for VLSI design. In *Machine learning* (pp. 271-289).

14. Beerel, P. A., & Pedram, M. (2018, May). Opportunities for machine learning in electronic design automation. In *2018 IEEE International Symposium on Circuits and Systems (ISCAS)* (pp. 1-5). IEEE.

15. Ioannides, C., & Eder, K. I. (2012). Coverage-directed test generation automated by machine learning--a review. *ACM Transactions on Design Automation of Electronic Systems (TODAES), 17*(1), 1-21.

16. Wang, F., Zhu, H., Popli, P., Xiao, Y., Bodgan, P., & Nazarian, S. (2018, May). Accelerating coverage directed test generation for functional verification: A neural network-based framework. In *Proceedings of the 2018 on Great Lakes Symposium on VLSI* (pp. 207-212).

17. Stratigopoulos, H. G., & Makris, Y. (2008). Error moderation in low-cost machine-learning-based analog/RF testing. *IEEE Transactions on Computer-Aided Design of Integrated Circuits and Systems, 27*(2), 339-351.

18. Biswas, S., & Blanton, R. D. (2006). Statistical test compaction using binary decision trees. *IEEE Design & Test of Computers, 23*(6), 452-462.

19. Wang, S., & Wei, W. (2009, April). Machine learning-based volume diagnosis. In *2009 Design, Automation & Test in Europe Conference & Exhibition* (pp. 902-905). IEEE.

20. Huang, Y., Benware, B., Klingenberg, R., Tang, H., Dsouza, J., & Cheng, W. T. (2017, November). Scan chain diagnosis based on unsupervised machine learning. In *2017 IEEE 26th Asian Test Symposium (ATS)* (pp. 225-230). IEEE.

21. Rahmani, K., Ray, S., & Mishra, P. (2016). Postsilicon trace signal selection using machine learning techniques. *IEEE Transactions on Very Large Scale Integration (VLSI) Systems, 25*(2), 570-580.

22. Kahng, A. B., Luo, M., & Nath, S. (2015, June). SI for free: machine learning of interconnect coupling delay and transition effects. In *2015 ACM/IEEE International Workshop on System Level Interconnect Prediction (SLIP)* (pp. 1-8). IEEE.

23. Medico, R., Spina, D., Ginste, D. V., Deschrijver, D., & Dhaene, T. (2019). Machine-learning-based error detection and design optimization in signal integrity applications. *IEEE Transactions on Components, Packaging and Manufacturing Technology, 9*(9), 1712-1720.

24. Fang, Y. C., Lin, H. Y., Su, M. Y., Li, C. M., & Fang, E. J. W. (2018, November). Machine-learning-based dynamic IR drop prediction for ECO. In *Proceedings of the International Conference on Computer-Aided Design* (pp. 1-7).

25. Ding, D., Torres, A. J., Pikus, F. G., & Pan, D. Z. (2011, January). High performance lithographic hotspot detection using hierarchically refined machine learning. In *16th Asia and South Pacific Design Automation Conference (ASP-DAC 2011)* (pp. 775-780). IEEE.

26. Geng, H., Yang, H., Yu, B., Li, X., & Zeng, X. (2018, July). Sparse VLSI layout feature extraction: A dictionary learning approach. In *2018 IEEE Computer Society Annual Symposium on VLSI (ISVLSI)* (pp. 488-493). IEEE.

27. Ram, O. S., & Saurabh, S. (2020). Modeling multiple-input switching in timing analysis using machine learning. *IEEE Transactions on Computer-Aided Design of Integrated Circuits and Systems*, 40(4), 723-734.

28. Wang, L. C., & Abadir, M. S. (2014, June). Data mining in EDA-basic principles, promises, and constraints. In *2014 51st ACM/EDAC/IEEE Design Automation Conference (DAC)* (pp. 1-6). IEEE.

29. Capodieci, Luigi. "Data analytics and machine learning for continued semiconductor scaling." *SPIE News* (2016).

30. Wang, L. C. (2016). Experience of data analytics in EDA and test—Principles, promises, and challenges. *IEEE Transactions on Computer-Aided Design of Integrated Circuits and Systems*, 36(6), 885-898.

31. Pandey, M. (2018, January). Machine learning and systems for building the next generation of EDA tools. In *2018 23rd Asia and South Pacific Design Automation Conference (ASP-DAC)* (pp. 411-415). IEEE.

32. Kahng, A. B. (2018, March). Machine learning applications in physical design: Recent results and directions. In *Proceedings of the 2018 International Symposium on Physical Design* (pp. 68-73).

33. Tripathi, S.L., Saxena, S., & Mohapatra, S.K. (Eds.). (2020). *Advanced VLSI Design and Testability Issues* (1st ed.). CRC Press Boca Raton. https://doi.org/10.1201/9781003083436

34. Suman Lata Tripathi, Sobhit Saxena, Sanjeet Kumar Sinha and Govind Singh Patel (2021) *Digital VLSI Design Problems and Solution with Verilog*, John Wiley & Sons, Ltd. DOI:10.1002/9781119778097 ISBN: 978-1-119-77804-2.

4

IoT-Based Smart Home Security Alert System for Continuous Supervision

Rajeswari[1]*, N. Vinod Kumar[1], K. M. Suresh[1], N. Sai Kumar[1]
and K. Girija Sravani[2]†

*¹Department of ECE, Lakireddy Bali Reddy College of Engineering,
Mylavaram, India*
²Department of ECE, KL University, Green Fields, Guntur, Andhra Pradesh, India

Abstract

Before the introduction of the Internet of Things (IoT), the involvement of manpower was more involved in providing security to the home. Even with the right involvement of manpower, it is difficult to identify unusual events like fire accidents, gas leakage, and motion or presence of an intruder. The Internet of Things is a technology in which all devices communicate with each other through the internet. This technology can be used in our home security systems in an effective manner. Many existing systems failed to meet some challenging issues like multi-sensing operations, delay in alerts and non-continuous monitoring due to power breakdowns. In this paper, we developed an IoT-based smart security alert system which is used to send alerts to the owner through SMS and email whenever there is an intruder or other harmful activities are taking place at the home. This system mainly consists of Raspberry Pi-3, Pi camera, power shifting circuit, gas sensor, fire sensor, IR sensor, Ultrasonic sensor, GSM module, Buzzer and mobile. In the proposed system, whenever any intruder is detected the system will capture an image and alert the user by sending SMS and email to the user. It also provides security regarding fire and smoke by sending SMS to the user. Our proposed system is also equipped with a power shifter circuit which provides continuous supply to the circuit for continuous monitoring.

Keywords: Raspberry Pi-3, Pi camera, GSM module, Internet of Things, home security, mobile

Corresponding author: rajewari.t1@gmail.com
†*Corresponding author*: kondavitee.sravani03@gmail.com

Abhishek Kumar, Suman Lata Tripathi, and K. Srinivasa Rao (eds.) Machine Learning for VLSI Chip Design, (51–64) © 2023 Scrivener Publishing LLC

4.1   Introduction

Nowadays, safety and security are two of the most important things in our day-to-day life. This includes security to the home, which is one of the major problems [1]. For every homeowner there is anxiety about the security of their house whenever they are not at home. Due to an increase in burglary and other unusual activities at home, security becomes very important. So there is a necessity to build an efficient security system which effectively manages all the problems, giving the the owner peace of mind about their home security in all situations.

A system is considered to be best only when it performs well in all kinds of situations by protecting their parameters. According to a report [2] by *India Today*, a burglary or robbery or house break-in happens in India every three minutes. So, it is necessary to make our home safe and secure.

An IoT-based smart home security alert system is the solution which reduces burglary activities at our home. In this system, some set of sensors will continuously monitor all the activities in and outside of the home. Whenever any intruder or suspicious activity is detected then the Raspberry-Pi module processes it and sends alerts to the homeowner. An email with the captured image is sent to the registered email id and SMS is sent to the registered mobile number. An AC and DC power altering circuit provides continuous power supply to the kit which makes it work continuously even in the case of main source fails [4, 5].

Raspberry Pi will act as a heart of the system because it performs all the necessary actions over the detected input by running the algorithm and producing the output as an information. It is transferred to the user in two ways:

1. SMS alerts
2. Email alerts

Here, SMS is transferred to the user by inserting a micro SIM in GSM module, and an email is sent to the user through the server over the internet.

IoT technology is used in this home security system. The IoT can be defined as a combination of physical devices which can communicate and share data with other physical devices over the internet [6].

Some of the drawbacks in the existing systems motivate us to provide a safe and more secure system which can detect any kind of burglary activities or any dangerous activities at home. The proposed system reduces all kind of threats that can cause more harm to the home. People need a security system which can inform the owner about troubling activities whenever they are away from home. By considering all the above points, the next section highlights the research contribution of this paper.

The contributions of this paper are as follows:

- The proposed architecture which provides security to the home in a smarter way by sending alerts to the owner through SMS and email.
- It can alert the owner and the necessary action can be taken immediately to solve that issue.
- The proposed system hardware is tested against different kinds of incidents like burglary, fire, and gas leakage.

The remaining part of the paper is as follows: section 4.2 is a literature survey of the proposed system. Section 4.3 describes the architecture and the components used in the proposed system and the working of the proposed system and its implementation. Finally, section 4.4 presents the results and concludes this paper.

4.2 Literature Survey

A home security system using IoT for detecting an intruder using PIR sensor and camera module by sending email alerts to the owner through Raspberry Pi module [1, 2] has a drawback of uni-functional detecting system and alert system. This can be resolved by using the multifunctional detecting and dual alert system which is implemented in the proposed system.

A smart home security monitoring system provides home automation and monitoring through motion sensor. It sends detailed home information to the user by sending SMS to the owner [3, 4] but has a drawback of interruption in monitoring due to power breakdowns. This can be solved by providing dual power shifting circuit in the system.

An IoT-based home security system using Raspberry Pi sends the alerts to the owner with some time delay over the internet [5–8] and it can be resolved by using a GSM module which is connected to the Raspberry Pi to reduce the time delay while sending alerts to the owner [9–12].

4.3 Results and Discussions

Most of the existing systems use the Raspberry Pi module, GSM module and a single functional sensor in their work to provide security to the home [3]. But most of the systems have some drawbacks:

- Uni-functional security and monitoring system.
- Interruption in monitoring due to power breakdowns.
- Non-web cam enabled system.

According to a literature survey [3] by NCRB in 2017, various types of crimes are involved in stolen property; these are shown in the below Figure 4.1.

In this proposed system, various sensors are used, like Fire, Smoke sensors which detect the fire, gas leakage accidents, process it in Raspberry Pi and send the SMS to the mobile through the GSM module. IR and Ultrasonic sensors are used to detect the burglary activities at the home and alerts are sent to the owner by sending captured images through email over the internet. This entire system works with two power sources: one is AC power supply and the other is DC power supply. The power source is altered in case of power shutdowns for continuous monitoring.

The architecture of the proposed system is shown below in Figure 4.2.

Various components are used in the proposed system as follows.

4.3.1 Raspberry Pi-3 B+Module

Raspberry Pi module acts as processor in which each and every operation can be processed in a quick manner by running the algorithm over the

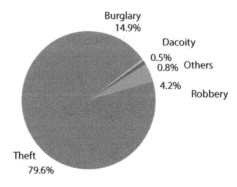

Figure 4.1 Various types of crimes involved in stolen property reported by NCRB.

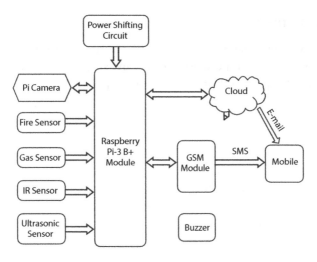

Figure 4.2 Architecture of smart home security alert system.

operation. It acts as an intermediate between the sensors and actuators. All the remaining components in the proposed system are interconnected to the Raspberry Pi module. The Raspberry Pi contains Broadcom BCM2835 System on Chip (SOC) module. The SOC's performance is equivalent to an old smartphone. By default, the Raspberry Pi module is operating at 700 MHZ. It also contains power source pin, 1 LAN port, 4 USB ports, SD card, HDMI port, 40 GPIO pins, DSI connector, audio jack, video connector, status LEDs, Ethernet and CSI port. The power source pin is used to provide power supply to the board, and an SD card is used to store the data in the processor. GPIO pins are used to connect the input and output ports. Status LEDs are used to display the status of the various activities in the system. CSI port is used to connect the PI camera module to the processor. Normal microprocessors cannot have the additional features like Raspberry Pi-3 B+ module [8].

Figure 4.3 Pi camera module.

4.3.2   Pi Camera

The Pi Camera module is used to capture the image of intruder or object whenever IR or Ultrasonic sensor senses any suspicious activity. It is connected to the Raspberry Pi at the CSI port (Figure 4.3).

4.3.3   Relay

Relays is a hardware device which is used to get a single power supply by applying dual power supplies as their inputs. It is used to provide continuous monitoring to the home in case of power breakdowns. It acts as a switch between AC and DC power supply. It alters the AC and DC supply whenever either one fails.

4.3.4   Power Source

The dual supply power source is used to avoid the power breakdowns in the system. A transformer is used to filter the main power supply (AC) and a 5V DC power source is used to manage the interruption in power supply.

4.3.5   Sensors

Various sensors used in the proposed system are as follows.

4.3.5.1   IR & Ultrasonic Sensor

IR and ultrasonic sensors are used to detect the object or intruder at home. But specifically, an Ultrasonic sensor is used to measure the distance between the intruder and the sensor. The IR sensor contains transmitter and receiver. It transmits a light when any object is detected and it returns the light to the receiver. An ultrasonic sensor is basically a 4-pin module which contains VCC, Trigger, Echo and Ground, respectively. It is used to find the distance between the intruder and the sensor. The work of the ultrasonic sensor is to transmit an ultrasonic wave when it objected by any object it returns to the receiver. We can calculate the distance by using ultrasonic sensor simply using a formulae, Distance = speed * time.

4.3.5.2   Gas Sensor

It is a hardware device which is used to detect smoke and gases like LPG, Hydrogen, CO and even methane in the home. When any gas is detected, it sends the data to the Raspberry Pi.

4.3.5.3   Fire Sensor

It is a hardware device which is used to detect fire accidents at home. Whenever any fire is detected at home, the fire sensor sends the data to Raspberry Pi.

4.3.5.4   GSM Module

It acts as a bridge between the Raspberry Pi and the end user to transfer SMS alerts to the registered mobile. It stands for Global System for Mobile Communication. In this we are using SIM900A module which contains a micro sim to transfer SMS to the user. It transfers SMS to the user whenever any unusual incidents happen at home.

4.3.5.5   Buzzer

It is a hardware device which is used to alert the owner or neighborhood whenever any burglary/unusual activities happen.

4.3.5.6   Cloud

The VNC viewer is an application which is used to connect with the internet. It is an open-source IoT (Internet of Things) server which interacts with the Raspberry Pi module and registered IP address mobile [4]. We can view the algorithm behind this system through this application. It acts as a database where the data is stored over the cloud and it gets analyzed and displays the task it performed.

4.3.5.7   Mobile

It acts as an interface between the system and user to alert the user through SMS and email which is sent by the system with the help of VNC viewer app over the server. The algorithm contains the registered mobile number and email id to where the alerts have to be sent. We can use a smartphone to check the messages and email alerts sent by the system. The user can take necessary action upon receiving alerts from the system. Whenever any sensor senses any activity the SMS will be displayed as "Abnormal condition" in mobile. The Pi cam captures the image and sends it to the registered email through the server [2].

The hardware setup of the proposed system is as shown in Figure 4.4.

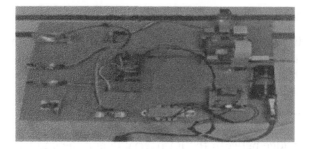

Figure 4.4 Hardware setup of proposed system.

The working and implementation of an IoT-based smart home security alert system starts from detecting an unusual event at home and continues until the user receives the alerts from the system, as shown in Figure 4.5.

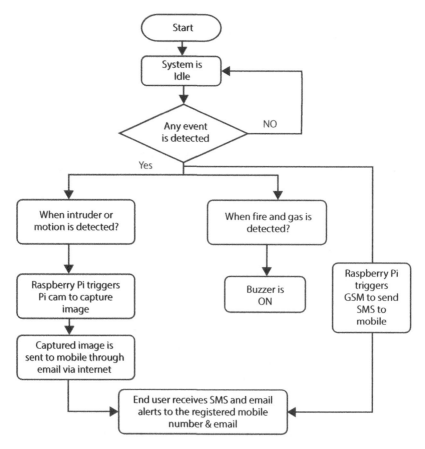

Figure 4.5 Flow chart of proposed system.

The system remains in idle state whenever any unusual activities are not detected. When any event is detected then the sensors sense the particular activity and send the data to the Raspberry Pi module. When any fire and gas leakage is detected, the Raspberry Pi activates the buzzer and sends the SMS to the registered mobile through GSM module. When any intruder or motion is detected, the Raspberry Pi module triggers the Pi cam to capture the image and it sends the captured image to the registered email over the cloud [1]. To avoid interruption in monitoring, a dual power supply is used when the main source fails. Finally, the end user receives both SMS and email alerts to their mobile at any place over the internet.

To fix the proposed system to the cloud some steps have to be taken. The following are the steps that should be taken while connecting system over the cloud:

1. Set up all the hardware connections in the system to Raspberry Pi module and connect it to the monitor/laptop.
2. Download and install VNC viewer application in the laptop to configure the system to the laptop.
3. Connect the server to the system by entering the IP address of the registered mobile/Ethernet which provides internet to the system.
4. Open the program file in Python shell which we have already placed into the Raspberry Pi SD memory.
5. Run the code and observe the simulation results in the Viewer window.
6. If any event is detected by the sensors then it performs the task and sends the alerts to the registered number and email which we have given in the program. Once it get executed then it continues the process until the system is off.

The results for the proposed system are shown in Figures 4.5, 4.6, and 4.7. The proposed system also contains the power altering circuit which avoids power loss in the system and is tested under different scenarios, such as:

- When fire is detected at home
- When gas leakage is detected at home
- When any intruder or motion is detected

Scenario 1: When fire is detected at home.

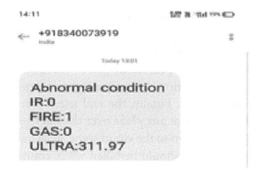

Figure 4.6 SMS alert to mobile when fire is detected.

When fire is detected at home then the Raspberry Pi activates the GSM module to send SMS to registered mobile number and also a buzzer is activated to alert the neighbors.

Scenario 2: When gas leakage is detected at home.

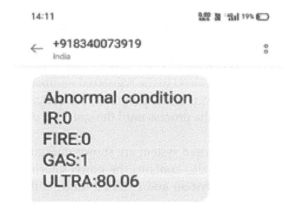

Figure 4.7 SMS alert to mobile when any gas leakage is detected.

When any gas leakage is detected at the home, the Raspberry Pi activates the GSM module to send an SMS to the registered mobile number and also a buzzer is activated to alert the neighbors (Figure 4.8).

Scenario 3: When any intruder or motion is detected.

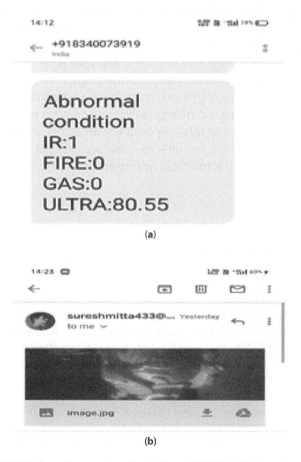

Figure 4.8 (a) SMS alert when any intruder is detected, (b) E-mail alert when any intruder is detected.

When any intruder or motion is detected at home then the Raspberry Pi activates the GSM module to send SMS to registered mobile number and triggers the PI camera to capture the image of the intruder and sends the image to the registered email over the internet.

4.4   Conclusions

This paper provides the solution for the drawbacks in the existing systems by implementing an IoT-based smart home security alert system. This system improves the performance of home security by providing multi-sensing operations, auto power switching and dual alert systems like SMS and email. Raspberry Pi has the capabilities to connect with other devices in an easier way. The technology used in this system which is IoT (Internet of Things) is a fast-growing technology at present and it has more scope in the future. The future scope of this proposed system is that it can be extended to any kind of application, not only to home security but also automation and security by making some small improvements in the system.

References

1. R. G. Anvekar and R. M. Banakar, "IoT application development: Home security system," *2017 IEEE Technological Innovations in ICT for Agriculture and Rural Development (TIAR)*, **2017**, pp. 68-72, doi: 10.1109/ TIAR.2017.8273688.
2. Tanwar, S., Patel, P., Patel, K., Tyagi, S., Kumar, N., & Obaidat, M. S. (2017), "An advanced Internet of Thing based Security Alert System for Smart Home", *2017 International Conference on Computer, Information and Telecommunication Systems (CITS)*. doi:10.1109/cits.2017.8035326.
3. Ray, A. K., & Bagwari, A. (2020), "IoT based Smart home Security Aspects and security architecture", *2020 IEEE 9th International Conference on Communication Systems and NetworkTechnologies CSNT)*. doi:10.1109/ csnt48778.2020.9115737.
4. Hong, X., Yang, C., & Rong, C., "Smart Home Security Monitor System," *2016 15th International Symposium on Parallel and Distributed Computing (ISPDC)*. doi:10.1109/ispdc.2016.42.
5. R. K. Kodali, V. Jain, S. Bose and L. Boppana, "IoT based smart security and home automation system," *International Conference on Computing, Communication and Automation (ICCCA)*, **2016**, pp. 1286-1289, doi: 10.1109/CCAA.2016.7813916.
6. R. K. Kodali, S. C. Rajanarayanan, A. Koganti and L. Boppana, "IoT based security system," *TENCON 2019 - 2019 IEEE Region 10 Conference (TENCON)*, **2019**, pp. 1253-1257, doi: 10.1109/TENCON.2019.8929420.
7. A. Pawar and V. M. Umale, "Internet of Things Based Home Security Using Raspberry Pi," *2018 Fourth International Conference on Computing Communication Control and Automation (ICCUBEA)*, **2018**, pp. 1-6, doi: 10.1109/ICCUBEA.2018.8697345.

8. S. Somani, P. Solunke, S. Oke, P. Medhi and P. P. Laturkar, "IoT Based Smart Security and Home Automation," *2018 Fourth International Conference on Computing Communication Control and Automation (ICCUBEA)*, **2018**, pp. 1-4, doi: 10.1109/ICCUBEA.2018.8697610.

9. S. A. I. Quadri and P. Sathish, "IoT based home automation and surveillance system," *2017 International Conference on Intelligent Computing and Control Systems (ICICCS)*, **2017**, pp. 861-866, doi: 10.1109/ICCONS.2017.8250586.

10. S. Supriya, R. Charanya and S. J. Madhumitha, "A Review On Home Automation System Using IOT," *2020 International Conference on Emerging Trends in Information Technology and Engineering (ic-ETITE)*, **2020**, pp. 1-11, doi: 10.1109/ic-ETITE47903.2020.363.

11. Sehgal, K., & Singh, R. (2019). "Iot Based Smart Wireless Home Security Systems", **2019** *3rd International Conference on Electronics, Communication and Aerospace Technology (ICECA)*. doi:10.1109/iceca.2019.8821885

12. Lata Tripathi, S., & Dwivedi, S. (Eds.). (2022). *Electronic Devices and Circuit Design: Challenges and Applications in the Internet of Things* (1st ed.). Apple Academic Press. https://doi.org/10.1201/9781003145776. **ISBN:** 9781771889933

5

A Detailed Roadmap from Conventional-MOSFET to Nanowire-MOSFET

P. Kiran Kumar[1,2*], B. Balaji[1], M. Suman[1], P. Syam Sundar[1], E. Padmaja[2] and K. Girija Sravani[1]

*Department of ECE, Koneru Lakshmaiah Educational Foundation
(Deemed to be University), Guntur, Andhra Pradesh, India*
Department of ECE, Balaji Institute of Technology, Narasampet, Warangal, India

Abstract

Recently, the need for low-power, high-speed portable devices grew rapidly in the semiconductor industry. The developments in process technology made development of transistors with reduced dimensions, which led to the growth of the number of transistors on ICs. Also, the scaling of transistors along with CMOS technology made continuous upgrading of speed and power consumption of ICs. The scaled down transistor in the sub-100nm regime causes Short Channel Effects (SCE) such as lowering barrier height by drain supply, gate leakage, higher sub-threshold conduction and poly depletion, etc., and the effects of these are reduced by usage of various engineering techniques like metal work function, channel-doping profile and gate oxide. In the sub-45nm regime, the controllability on the channel is enhanced by introducing a new structure Thin-body SOI MOSFET with single and double gate. At 22nm nanometer technology, another new structure Fin-FET is proposed for further enhancement of controllability of gate on the channel. The Fin-FET utilizes double-gate, tri-gate, pi-gate, and omega-gate structures for further improvement of controllability. Further scaling down of MOSFETs to sub-10nm, the GAA nanowire-MOSFET exhibits better SCE immunity as compared to Fin-FETs. In this survey, we discuss the challenges in conventional MOSFET, advantages and limitations of Thin-body SOI-MOSFET, Fin-FET and various approaches to design nanowire-MOSFET in the sub-5nm regime. It is observed that the nanowire-MOSFETs have lower leakage and higher drive current as compared to other MOSFET structures at sub-5nm regime.

Corresponding author: kiranpadakanti0430@gmail.com

Abhishek Kumar, Suman Lata Tripathi, and K. Srinivasa Rao (eds.) Machine Learning for VLSI
Chip Design, (65–94) © 2023 Scrivener Publishing LLC

Keywords: Short-channel-effects, scaling challenges, thin-body SOI-MOSFET, Fin-FET, nanowire-MOSFET

5.1 Introduction

Silicon-based micro-electronic devices have changed human life in the last several decades and continue to have an extraordinary impact on all aspects of life today [1–3]. Such electronic devices and systems are used in a variety of applications including telecommunications, warfare, defense, medical, energy conservation, industrial automation, transportation, autonomous vehicles, amusement, infotainment, and the digital society [2–4]. The revolutionary changes in micro-electronics were experienced after fabrication of bipolar-junction-transistors [5, 6] and they further increased after the development of the first working ICs [7, 8]. Further, the development of MOSFET device and fabrication of amplifier with MOSFET allowed for integration of huge number of transistors along with connections on a single semiconductor wafer at lower cost [9, 10] and this led to the formulation of complementary-MOS (CMOS) device structure with pMOS and nMOS transistor for two-input and one-output inverter configuration [11]. In 1965, Gordon Moore predicted that the number of devices placed on a wafer would double every two years, and this prediction later became known as "Moore's law" [12]. Moore's rule was based on the premise that smaller devices enhance practically every element of IC functioning, especially lower cost and switching power consumption per transistor, as well as increased speed and memory capacity.

The growing need for battery-powered portable devices necessitated the development of electronic equipment that were operated with higher operating speed, lower power consumption, and were tiny in size. Each successive generation of IC technology has resulted in cheaper cost, higher device density, reduction in power consumption, and enhancement in processing speed IC-chips by scaling down device footprints according to scaling principles [13]. As per the scaling rule of MOSFET [13], as length of the channel (Lg) is reduced, then the oxide thickness is correspondingly reduced to maintain the same capacitive coupling between the gate terminal and inversion channel in relation to the other transistor terminals. As the scaling process is continued, the Short-Channel-Effects (SCEs) such as subthreshold swing (SS) deterioration, Hot Carrier Effects, Velocity saturation, threshold voltage (Vth) roll-off, and Drain-Induced Barrier Lowering (DIBL) are enabled, and the influence of these SCEs is severe when channel length is scaled down to beyond 100nm [14, 15]. In addition, along with the reduction in Lg there is a corresponding increment in the body doping (Nb) and a decrement in the source-drain junction depth Xj to reduce the subsurface leak path under the channel inversion layer. At each new technological node, the worldwide effort to miniaturize MOSFETs and circuit optimization in CMOS technology continues to produce ICs with higher computational speed, lower-power consumption, and lower cost [16, 17].

The US Semiconductor Industry Association (SIA) created the National Technology Roadmap for Semiconductors (NTRS) in 1994 and transitioned to the International Technology Roadmap for Semiconductors (ITRS) in 2000 by including global semiconductor companies in order to continue Moore's law device miniaturization. Following Moore's law and Dennard's scaling rule, the ITRS set extensive criteria for future generations of technology. For multiple generations of VLSI technology, this scaling process has proven to be quite effective. However, due to insurmountable obstacles, standard MOSFET scaling methods could no longer provide positive advances in device performance established by Moore's law for 100 nm planar-CMOS technology and beyond [14, 15]. In this paper we have discussed a couple of engineering techniques that have been developed to minimize SCEs in shorter length channels. The engineering techniques fall into classifications like Channel Engineering, Gate Oxide Engineering and Device Engineering, etc.

The remainder of the paper is organized in the following manner. The hardships experienced by Bulk-MOSFETs due to scaling of channel length are discussed in Section 5.2. Section 5.3 discusses the alternative concepts for conventional-MOSFETs. Section 5.4 examines the Thin-Body SOI-MOSFETS's advantages and disadvantages with single and double gate over Bulk-MOSFETs. Section 5.5 demonstrates the non-planar structure of Fin-FET, advantages as well as its limitations. Section 5.6 focuses on another non-planar architecture of nanowire-MOSFET and various engineering techniques used to enhance its performance. The conclusion of this paper is discussed in Section 5.7.

5.2   Scaling Challenges Beyond 100nm Node

The worsening of leakage current is the most significant limitation to MOSFET device scaling in the sub-100 nanometer regime. The performance of MOSFET devices becomes increasingly reliant on gate length when they are scaled down to the nanoscale regime [18, 19]. As per the scaling rule, the bulk doping concentration is enhanced to prevent source-drain punch-through and subsurface leakage current when Lg is decreased.

Because of the increased vertical electric field caused by enhancement in bulk doping concentration resulted in decrement in the mobility of the carrier and deterioration of the drive current in scaled devices. In addition to that, the increment in the band-to-band tunneling caused by high vertical electric field resulted in increment in the leakage current. Consequently, reduction in the gate length of MOSFET in the nanometer regime deteriorates the MOSFET characteristics, subthreshold slope and also lowers the threshold voltage (Vth) results Vth roll-off [20].

As demonstrated in Figure 5.1, regulating the leakage current in scaled devices is a critical challenge for continuous scaling of traditional bulk-MOSFETs. The noticed leakage current in downsized devices at nanoscale nodes is predominantly caused by leakage channels many nanometers underneath the silicon/gate-dielectric contact [19]. To continue scaling of MOSFETs at the nanoscale node, tremendous efforts on channel engineering, shallow source-drain extensions (SSDE), and halo implants surrounding SSDEs [21–26] were made. However, for regular MOSFET structures beyond the 45 nm regime, the subsurface leakage current is unable to control by reducing gate-oxide thickness to as small as possible [19] and it led to development of new structures.

According to Roy *et al.* [14], there is considerable leakage current in deep-sub micrometer regimes as gate oxide thickness and gate length are lowered. When the gate length is lowered, SCEs such as weak inversion,

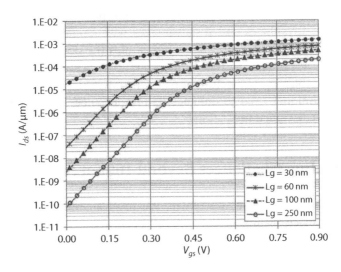

Figure 5.1 Drain current (I_{ds}) versus gate voltage (V_{gs}) characteristics of the conventional n-MOSFET [19].

Drain-Induced-Barrier-Lowering (DIBL), Gate-Induced-Drain-Leakage (GIDL), hot carrier injection, and gate oxide tunneling become sources of leakage currents. At the nanoscale node planar-MOSFET technology, there is a possibility of two ways for overcoming the scaling limits described above in traditional MOSFETs. The first approach is to incorporate new techniques, materials and doping methods into traditional planar MOSFETs in order to enable further reduction of device dimensions and performance improvement in scaled devices [27, 28]. Alternative device topologies, such as ultrathin-body MOSFETs and multiple-gate MOSFETs, provide greater electrostatic control over the inverted channel intrinsically [1, 19], as detailed in the next sections.

5.3   Alternate Concepts in MOFSETs

During the past two decades efforts have been made in research and development to explore alternate device topologies [1, 19, 29–34] for VLSI fabrication technology at nanoscale nodes in order to solve the rising hurdles in continuous reduction of device dimensions in traditional planar MOSFET devices. As illustrated in Figure 5.2 [35], Fujita *et al.* presented improved channel engineering to construct nanoscale MOSFET devices with un-doped/lightly-doped channels to reduce the influence of Random-Discrete-Doping. Conventional CMOS processing techniques are used to construct the channel on an intrinsic epitaxial-layer which is formed on a silicon substrate [35]. This type of MOSFET construction is called as Deeply-depleted-channel (DDC) MOSFETs [35]. The advantage of DDC

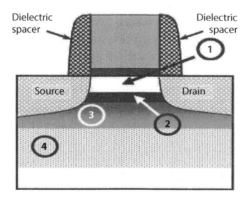

Figure 5.2 Deeply-depleted-channel MOSFET: In the schematic, region 1 is the undoped channel.

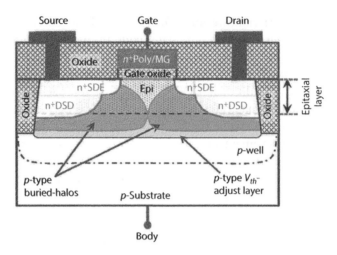

Figure 5.3 Buried-halo MOSFET device [37].

device is decrement in Channel-Drain coupling capacitance due to highly doped channel layers 2 & 3 resulting in reduction of subsurface leakage current, and the process variability is controlled with the un-doped/lightly-doped channel [35]. The structure of the device is shown in Figure 5.2.

Further, Saha *et al.* designed halo doping around Source-Drain of the MOSFET to decrease subsurface OFF-state current. The halo doping refers to combining a lightly doped channel with highly doped implant. This double halo MOSFETs consisting of two halo doping profiles decreases the OFF-state current with the proper adjustment of threshold voltage in nanometer devices [1, 24–26]. This device architecture is also called as "buried-halo MOSFET (BH-MOSFET)". In the fabrication of BH-MOSFET, halo doping profiles are implanted in the silicon substrate for the adjustment of threshold voltage. These processing steps are performed before the formation of the channel layer by epitaxy method. After epitaxy layer formation source drain regions as well as gate patterning is done [36, 37], which is illustrated in Figure 5.3. In comparison to traditional MOSFET devices, from the data available on threshold voltage variability, it is understood that there is a considerable decrement in threshold voltage variation because of Random-Discrete-Doping in nanometer BH-MOSFETs [1, 37].

5.4 Thin-Body Field-Effect Transistors

An alternative device structure used to reduce major OFF-state leakage current in the channel as compared to traditional MOSFET is

Silicon-On-Insulator MOSFET [38–40] and these are also called as Thin-Body MOSFETs. This device uses thin-body silicon as the channel, and it is the unique feature in the architecture of the device that ensures higher gate control of the channel for MOSFET devices. Placing of Ultrathin-silicon as the body on SOI-substrate and controlling of Ultrathin-silicon body using multiple gates [19] in different directions are the two techniques used to improve the controllability of the gate and decrease the drain controllability on the channel and Drain-Channel coupling capacitance.

5.4.1   Single-Gate Ultrathin-Body Field-Effect Transistor

As seen in Figures 5.4 and 5.5, the SOI devices are classified into two types, taking the silicon film thickness (tSi) into consideration. If the tSi is greater than the depletion width around Source/Drain then area of the channel is partially depleted, and this type of SOI device structure is referred to as a Partially Depleted (PD) SOI device. The region of the channel which is below the inversion layer is totally depleted when tSi is lesser than the depletion width, resulting in a Fully Depleted (FD) SOI device. The use of an ultrathin SOI substrate is to put silicon closer to the gate [41] and this can considerably reduce SCEs in MOSFETs. However, the device parameters such as thickness of silicon film, gate-oxide thickness, and doping concentration of body controls the SCEs in SOI substrate MOSFETs. From the literature, it is observed that the OFF-state current reduces when thickness of silicon film decreases [42, 43]. SCEs can be greatly reduced by lowering thickness of silicon film to roughly 7 to 14 nm, and it leads to end of leakage paths at buried oxide layer in SOI MOSFETs as shown in Figure 5.6 [42, 43]. The greater mobility in SOI MOSFET transistors leads to a large increase in ON-state current over a typical traditional MOSFETs [44]. SOI MOSFETs have lower parasitic junction capacitances, which accelerates

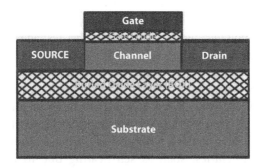

Figure 5.4 Fully depleted (FD) SOI-MOSFET.

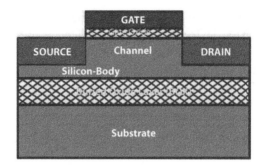

Figure 5.5 Partially depleted (PD) SOI-MOSFET.

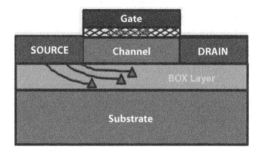

Figure 5.6 Ultrathin-body SOI-MOSFETs with termination of leakage paths in buried-oxide.

the ON-state current and allows them to be faster than their bulk silicon MOSFETs [44]. There are two parasitic components, bulk capacitance and drain-channel coupling capacitance in traditional bulk-MOSFETs whereas SOI MOSFET contains only drain-channel coupling capacitance because of end of leakage lines at buried oxide layer which lead to decrement of parasitic capacitance in SOI MOSFET as compared to bulk-MOSFET.

Furthermore, SOI MOSFETs are low-power devices due to their reduced inverse subthreshold, which allows for the usage of devices with lower threshold voltages without an increase in leakage current as compared to bulk-MOSFET devices with lengthy gate lengths [45]. This significantly minimizes static power usage. Additionally, using Ultrathin-Body MOSFETs on an intrinsic or weakly doped substrate lowers variability. UTB-SOI-MOSFETs have emerged as one of the most promising devices for advanced VLSI circuits at the nanoscale node [42, 43, 47–49].

Although SOI devices have numerous advantages, they also have certain reliability difficulties, such as self-heating due to insufficient heat dissipation [44]; thin film also causes hot-electron degradation [44], and floating-body effect in PD-SOI devices [44]. Thin SOI multi-gate MOSFET devices are particularly appealing beyond 32nm technology because of their outstanding electrostatic control and increased transport capabilities [46].

5.4.2   Multiple-Gate Ultrathin-Body Field-Effect Transistor

Usage of multiple gates around the channel or on the sides of the channel improves the controllability of the channel which leads to effective deterioration of SCEs; this is often called as multi-gate MOSFET devices. Figure 5.7 shows one type of multi-gate MOSFET with two gates placed at top and bottom of thin silicon body. For the Double-gate MOSFET structure illustrated in Figure 5.7, the sub-surface leaky lines far away from the top gate are nearer to the bottom gate and these are removed by the bottom gate which are caused by the top gate. Similarly, the subsurface leaky lines far away from the top gate are nearer to the bottom gate and these are removed by the bottom gate which are caused by the top gate. As a result, the gates top and bottom of the silicon body provide excellent controllability of the electrostatic inverted channel in a Doublegate-MOSFET, and it leads to reduction of SCEs. Therefore, the multi-gate MOSFETs scalability range is more as compared to planar bulk-MOSFET devices [50, 51].

In contrast to the conventional scaling principle, thin-body MOSFET structure which is shown in Figure 5.7 eliminates the need for high doping of the channel for deteriorating SCEs. The tuning of threshold voltage can done by adjusting channel doping concentration instead of adjustment of metal-gate workfunction [1, 18]. Further, the usage of less doping or intrinsic as channel in thin-body MOSFET decreases the random discrete doping in multi-gate MOSFETs and thus eliminates device performance fluctuation. Furthermore, less doping or intrinsic body reduces the channel average electric field, resulting in increased carrier mobility, lower

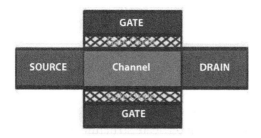

Figure 5.7 Ultrathin-body double-gate MOSFET.

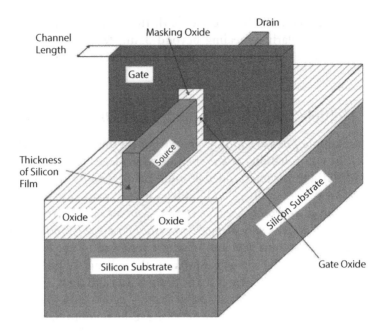

Figure 5.8 3-D ultrathin-body double-gate Fin-FET on silicon-on-insulator substrate.

OFF-state currents, and improved reliability of the device. This could help with the enhancement in the stability of bias temperature and deterioration of leakage tunneling current at gate-oxide [18].

Based on the foregoing, a thin-body double-gate MOSFET architecture, as illustrated in Figure 5.7, has a lot of potential for controlling SCEs and reducing OFF-state current as well as process variability by placing the gate near to the silicon body. Further, the rotation of double-gate MOSFET structure with 90 degrees forms a vertical double-gate MOSFET and it looks like placing MOSFET on silicon-substrate or SOI-substrate. The above said vertical double-gate MOSFET with thin fin-like body construction is called as FinFET as illustrated in Figure 5.8 and discussed in detail in the next section.

5.5   Fin-FET Devices

In terms of fabrication, among many MOSFET structures, Fin-FET architecture is the most viable multi-gate structure MOSFET. When compared to a conventional MOSFET device, this multi-gate thin-body device architecture has a higher resistance to SCE [1, 18]. In Fin-FET, the silicon sidewalls of the channel are controlled by the gate and it can be observed from three-dimensional Double-Gate FinFET architectures which are shown in Figures 5.8 and 5.9. The number of gates can be constructed along the sidewalls of the fin to increase the controllability of the channel in Fin-FET, and the number can be two, three or four. As the number of gates increases, fabrication complexity increases but higher electrostatic controllability of the channel can be achieved. Fin-FETs can be constructed on SOI-substrate as depicted in Figure 5.8 or on silicon-substrate as depicted in Figure 5.9. To construct Double-gate Fin-FET, the gate-dielectric is developed on either sides of the fin and dense masking-oxide is developed on fin-channel top, as can be observed from Figures 5.8 and 5.9. In the context of Triple-gate Fin-FET, the gate-dielectric is developed on either side of fin-channel as well as on the top of the fin-channel as shown in Figure 5.10. Therefore, the same thickness is used for either side of fin-channel and on the top of the fin-channel in triple-gate Fin-FETs.

In the subthreshold region, source-drain coupling is deteriorated in multi-gate Fin-FET, as the numerous gates constructed over the channel provide enhanced electrostatic control in the channel [52, 53]. The foremost thing is, an intrinsic channel is used in multi-gate FET which reduces the significant threat in process variability. Secondly, compared to

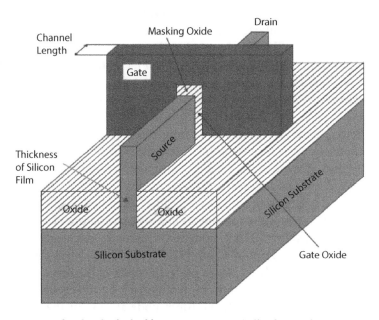

Figure 5.9 3-D ultrathin-body double-gate Fin-FET on bulk-silicon substrate.

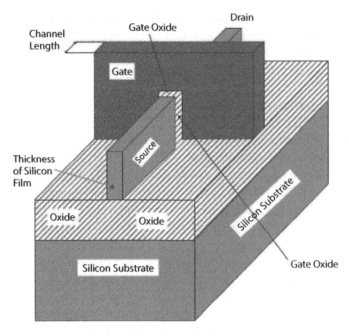

Figure 5.10 3-D ultrathin-body triple-gate Fin-FET on silicon-on-insulator substrate.

conventional MOSFET devices fabricated using 32 nm planar-CMOS technology, multi-gate MOSFETs offer lower OFF-state current by an order of four. Thus in the manufacturing of advanced nanoscale devices multi-gate FETs are used in VLSI technology [52–54].

For sub-22 nm node VLSI circuits, FINFET is the industry-standard CMOS technology [52, 54–56]. To produce tolerable SCEs in FinFETs, the length of the gate should be around three times the thickness of the fin-channel [57]. The threshold voltage in FinFET is reduced by keeping leakage current constant due to improvement in the performance of short-channel and it results in enhancement of drive current by higher overdrive gate-voltage. At 22nm and 14nm nodes, the subthreshold swing was 70mV/decade and 65mV/decade, respectively [52, 55]. The ON-State current per device can be enhanced by increasing height of the fins and decreasing the pitch of the fins due to quasi-planar nature of Fin-FET. As the device is scaled from 22-nm node to 14-nm node, the height of the fins was increased from 34 nm to 42 nm [52, 55]. Similarly, when the device is scaled from 22-nm node to 14-nm node, the pitch of the fins was reduced from 60 nm to 42 nm. The ratio of width of the fin to length of the gate was maintained constant up to 11/10nm node as 1/3. Further, the fabrication constraints added limitation on scaling of width of the fin to 6 nm.

The short channel exhibits degradation in the performance at 8 or 7nm node due to increment in ratio of width of the fin to length of the gate to 0.43. Furthermore, corner effects, contacted-Gate-pitch, complex fabrication process are the challenges faced due to further scaling of the FinFET devices, which lead to tradeoff in optimum performance of the device [58, 59].

5.6 GAA Nanowire-MOSFETS

The silicon nanowire-MOSFET has emerged as among the most promising choices for future large-scale integration due to rapid advancements in device downscaling [60, 61]. The next option for further scaling in the post Fin-FET era, i.e., beyond 7nm/5nm Fin-FET, is the Gate-All-Around (GAA) nanowire MOSFET shown in Figure 5.11. Even though the structure of the nanowire-MOSFET device is scaled down, strong electrostatic control by the gate terminal in the conduction channel is preserved [62, 63]. This phenomenon of excellent gate controllability of GAA nanowire-MOSFET made it a promising device for replacing Fin-FET in fast VLSI circuits. According to the reported data, compared to planar-MOSFET or Double-gate MOSFET structures, GAA nanowire-MOSFET scaling requirements are less stringent because wrapping the gate around channel enables efficient electrostatic control even at decreased natural length l [64–68]. Theoretical studies shows that there is no further improvement in Fin-FET as the device is scaled down from 7nm to 5nm because of weak controllability by the gate. At the same time, GAA nanowire-MOSFET is a strong contender for the technology nodes of sub-5nm [69]. The top-down fabrication approach in GAA nanowire-MOSFET is more attractive and more attentive because of Gate controllability on the channel, enhanced transport property, viable structure design support to scalability to the end of roadmap [70–76].

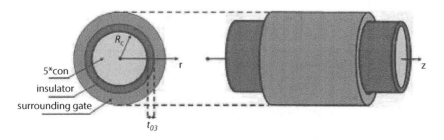

Figure 5.11 Gate-all-around nanowire-MOSFET.

A GAA nanowire-MOSFET is a semiconductor device in which the gate electrodes surround the device conducting channel in all directions [77, 78]. As a result, we have improved gate controllability over the device's channel. The GAA semiconductor device's channel form might be triangular, rectangular, square, or polygonal. The conducting channels of this nanowire-MOSFET can be n-channel nanowire MOSFET or p-channel nanowire-MOSFET. Various MOSFET device structures have been designed, which include silicon-on-insulator MOSFET, symmetric and asymmetric double-gate MOSFET, tri-gate MOSFET and Fin-FET. Among these, GAA device structures have demonstrated the advantage of strong gate control over channel [67, 79, 80]. It has the best electrical and conductivity qualities. In practice, "nanowires" are built on a planar substrate made of semiconductor materials such as silicon or germanium or compound materials [81–83].

The GAA nanowire-MOSFET structured devices are constructed in two configurations, namely Lateral nanowire-MOSFET (LFET) and Vertical nanowire-MOSFET (VFET). Kim *et al.* [84] designed LFET and VFET using 3D technology TCAD tools and the parasitic components corresponding to these MOSFETs are calculated by varying the diameter of the nanowire. Their overall parasitic resistance is categorized into contact-resistance, extension-resistance, sheet-resistance, and spreading-resistance, and overall parasitic capacitance is categorized into outer fringing-capacitance, overlap-capacitance, extension-capacitance, and inner fringing-capacitance [84]. The variation of these parasites with respect to variation of the diameter of the nanowire is depicted in Figures 5.12 and 5.13. The parasitic resistance in nanowire-MOSFET increases with the decrement of the diameter of the

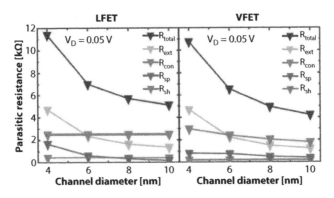

Figure 5.12 Parasitic resistance of lateral nanowire-MOSFET and vertical nanowire-MOSFET.

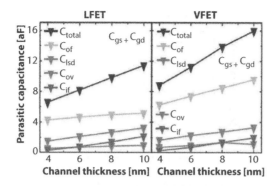

Figure 5.13 Parasitic capacitance of lateral nanowire-MOSFET and vertical nanowire-MOSFET.

nanowire because of increment in extension-resistance, whereas the parasitic capacitance in nanowire-MOSFET decreases with the decrement of the diameter of the nanowire [84]. When the parasites of VFET and LFET are compared, LFET has more parasitic resistance and VFET has more parasitic capacitance, which can be observed from Figures 5.14 and 5.15. The parasitic resistance difference between VFET and LFET is small, but the parasitic capacitance difference is higher, resulting in VFET having a longer delay than LFET [84].

Chenyun *et al.* [85] studied the performance of LFET and VFET at technology node of 5nm utilizing an ARM core CPU. The various device configurations such as nanowires, stacking of nanowires and different numbers of fins are investigated to find tradeoffs between area, frequency, energy and leakage by using multi-threshold optimization. The stress in the channel that may be induced in LFETs results in a higher ON-state

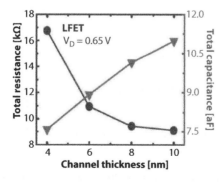

Figure 5.14 Resistance and capacitance of lateral nanowire-MOSFET during ON-state.

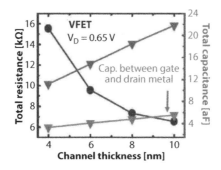

Figure 5.15 Resistance and capacitance of vertical nanowire-MOSFET during ON-state.

current; the results show that GAA LFET core has higher maximum frequency than its VFET equivalent [85]. The LFET GAA cores are hence advantageous for rapid timing targets [85]. When compared to LFET GAA cores with 2-stack/2-fin at the same leakage-current, the three nanowires VFET GAA cores offer a 20% energy saving and 7% area reduction for slow timing targets [85].

The nanowire MOSFET extension length tuning is presented by Kaushal *et al.* [86] as shown in Figure 5.16. The sub-14nm nanowire-MOSFET with tuning of extension length significantly reduces the power dissipation with a small active area; using of this in the 6-T nanowire SRAM cell improves the SRAM cell read stability. The device design parameters such as the diameter of the nanowire, the device extension length, source-drain doping and channel doping are utilized to improve the stability of the SRAM cells. The impact of these design parameters on ON-state and OFF-state

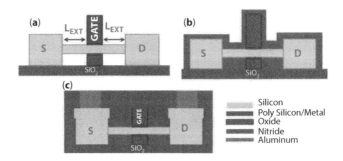

Figure 5.16 (a) silicon nanowire-MOSFET with extension, (b) silicon nanowire-MOSFET with extension and spacer, (c) silicon nanowire-MOSFET with extension, spacer and raised source-drain.

current for various extension lengths are studied [86] and depicted in Figures 5.17, 5.18 and 5.19. It is observed that the extension length tuning technique exhibits ~60% and 15% savings in static power consumption and active area [86], respectively, in comparison with a conventional nanowire-stack tuning technique. Furthermore, the hold and read noise margins are improved by 8% and 6% with the proposed technique, respectively.

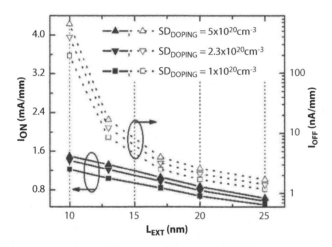

Figure 5.17 Source-drain doping concentration impact on ON-state current and OFF-state current.

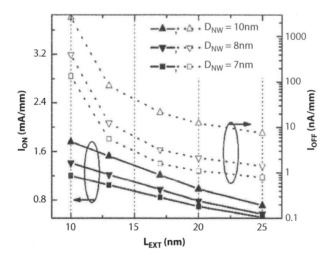

Figure 5.18 Diameter of the nanowire impact on ON-state current and OFF-state current.

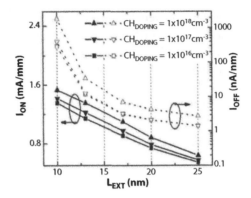

Figure 5.19 Channel doping concentration impact on ON-state current and OFF-state current.

The vertical nanowire-MOSFET with channel engineering is reported by Chen *et al.* [87] to achieve multi-threshold voltage. The usage of asymmetrical source halo doping or asymmetrical drain halo doping results in this multi-threshold voltage. The 3D and 2D cross-sectional view of asymmetrical source halo VFET is illustrated in Figure 5.20. By keeping the appropriate halo doping concentration, we can achieve at least three different threshold voltages and it also leads to controlling of leakage currents which can be observed from Figures 5.21 and 5.22. The results show that halo configuration close to source side exhibits larger threshold voltage tuning range and better SCE controlling [87]. Moreover, adjustment of halo doping concentration along with nanowire diameter can be a better

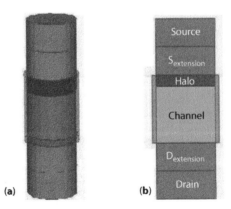

Figure 5.20 (a) 3-dimensional and (b) 2-dimensional view of source-halo vertical nanowire-MOSFET.

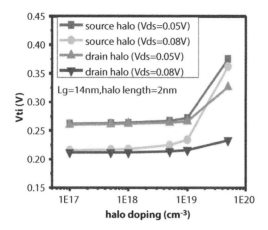

Figure 5.21 Impact of halo doping concentation on threshold voltage.

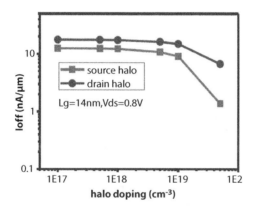

Figure 5.22 Impact of halo doping concentation on OFF-state current.

choice for proper adjustment of threshold voltage for 7nm technology node [87].

Further, Chen *et al.* [88] proposed asymmetric doping profile nanowire-MOSFET for enhancement of ON-state current. This VFET device utilizes extension region and spacer material with asymmetric doping profile as illustrated in Figure 5.23. The performance of this is analyzed for various spacer materials, spacer lengths as well as different doping profiles. As compared to lightly doped Source-drain and heavily doped Source-drain, Asymmetric-Graded-Lightly-Doped-Drain (AGLDD) exhibits higher ON-state current without affecting leakage as shown in Figures 5.24 and 5.25 [88]. Moreover, higher ON-state current

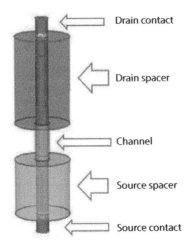

Figure 5.23 3-dimensional asymmetrical structure of vertical nanowire MOSFET.

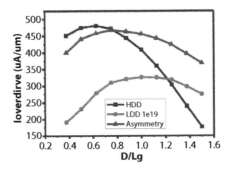

Figure 5.24 Impact of three varieties of doping profiles on ON-state current for various diameters of the nanowire.

and SCE immunity can be accomplished while parasitic capacitance can be kept within acceptable limits by using high-k spacer material and optimal drain spacer width [88]. This approach can be used to design low-power vertical channel nanowire FETs.

In addition, Goel *et al.* [89] proposed a Dual-Metal nanowire MOSFET (DM-NWFET) as shown in Figure 5.26. Two different work functions, i.e., a lower work function metal gate on the drain side and a higher work function metal gate on the source side is used in DM-NWFET. Dual metal was built using Molybdenum (Mo) as the gate material and its work function can be altered by manipulating the doping implant in Molybdenum [89].

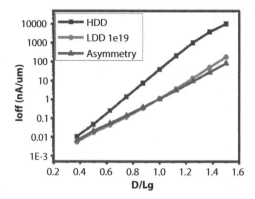

Figure 5.25 Impact of three varieties of doping profiles on OFF-state current for various diameters of the nanowire.

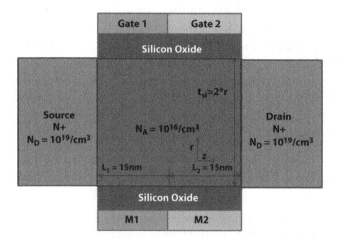

Figure 5.26 2-dimensional cross-sectional view dual metal nanowire-MOSFET.

GIDL is a leakage condition caused by minority carriers tunneling into the drain region. The applying of two different work functions causes deviation in the electric potential along the channel leading to the change in the electric field over the channel. The field aberration causes bending between the drain and gate regions, resulting in a release of minority carriers in the OFF-state as the GIDL current. Keeping the lower work function to the Gate2 in DM-NWFET decreases the velocity of electron and leads to reduction in tunneling of minority carriers during OFF-state. It therefore results in reduction of gate leakage [89–91].

5.7   Conclusion

In this review paper, we have observed the innovations in the structure of MOSFET as the device is scaled down to the sub-5nm node. Initially, as the MOSFET scaling reached to sub-100 nm regime, the channel in MOSFET is behaving like a short-channel which led to SCEs resulting in higher leakage current. It is overcome by an increase in the channel doping or usage of high-k oxides or usage of metal gate in conventional MOSFET. As the device is further scaled and reached to sub-45nm node, the severity in SCE is controlled by either single-gate thin-body SOI-MOSFET or double-gate thin-body SOI-MOSFET. At 22nm technology node, a new structure Fin-FET is proposed to overcome the limitations of SOI-MOSFETs, such as floating body, kink effect. The Fin-FET devices are constructed using multi-gate structures, i.e., double-gate, tri-gate, pi-gate, omega-gate and GAA, and the controllability on the channel is increased as we moved from double-gate to GAA. Furthermore, the GAA nanowire-MOSFETs are proposed due to their better electrical characteristics than Fin-FETs in the sub-10nm regime. The performance of conventional nanowire-MOSFETs is further improved by adding spacer material, extension layers, halo-doping and dual-metal. The nanowire-MOSFET exhibits lower leakage, higher drive current, near-ideal subthreshold swing and lower DIBL at sub-5nm regime as compared to other MOSFET structures.

References

1. Saha, S. K. (2015). Compact models for integrated circuit design: conventional transistors and beyond. Taylor & Francis.
2. Saha, S. K. (2018). Transitioning semiconductor companies enabling smart environments and integrated ecosystems. *Open Journal of Business and Management*, 6(2), 428-437.
3. Vermesan, O., Friess, P., Guillemin, P., Sundmaeker, H., Eisenhauer, M., Moessner, K., ... & Cousin, P. (2013). Internet of things strategic research and innovation agenda. In *Internet of things: converging technologies for smart environments and integrated ecosystems*, 7-152.
4. Saha, S. K. (2015). Emerging business trends in the microelectronics industry. *Open Journal of Business and Management*, 4(1), 105-113.
5. Shockley, W. (1998). Semiconductor Amplifier Patent. *Proceedings of the IEEE*, 86(1), 34-36.
6. Brattain, W. H., & Gibney, R. B. (1950). U.S. Patent No. 2,524,034. Washington, DC: U.S. Patent and Trademark Office.

7. Kilby, J. S. (2007). Miniaturized electronic circuits [US Patent no. 3,138, 743]. *IEEE Solid-State Circuits Society Newsletter*, 12(2), 44-54.
8. Kilby, J. S. (1976). Invention of the integrated circuit. *IEEE Transactions on Electron Devices*, 23(7), 648-654.
9. Kahng, D. (1960). Silicon-silicon dioxide field induced surface devices. In the Solid State Device Research Conf., Pittsburgh, PA. June 1960.
10. Dawon, K. (1963). U.S. Patent No. 3,102,230. Washington, DC: U.S. Patent and Trademark Office.
11. Wanlass, F. M. (1967). U.S. Patent No. 3,356,858. Washington, DC: U.S. Patent and Trademark Office.
12. Moore, G. E. (1965). Cramming more components onto integrated circuits.
13. Dennard, R. H., Gaensslen, F. H., Yu, H. N., Rideout, V. L., Bassous, E., & LeBlanc, A. R. (1974). Design of ion-implanted MOSFET's with very small physical dimensions. *IEEE Journal of solid-state circuits*, 9(5), 256-268.
14. Roy, K., Mukhopadhyay, S., & Mahmoodi-Meimand, H. (2003). Leakage current mechanisms and leakage reduction techniques in deep-submicrometer CMOS circuits. *Proceedings of the IEEE*, 91(2), 305-327.
15. Wong, H. S. (2002). Beyond the conventional transistor. *IBM Journal of Research and Development*, 46(2.3), 133-168.
16. Critchlow, D. L. (1999). MOSFET scaling-the driver of VLSI technology. *Proceedings of the IEEE*, 87(4), 659-667.
17. Kuhn, K. J. (2012). Considerations for ultimate CMOS scaling. *IEEE transactions on Electron Devices*, 59(7), 1813-1828.
18. Arora, N. D. (2012). *MOSFET models for VLSI circuit simulation: theory and practice*. Springer Science & Business Media.
19. Chauhan, Y. S., Lu, D., Venugopalan, S., Khandelwal, S., Duarte, J. P., Paydavosi, N., ... & Hu, C. (2015). *FinFET modeling for IC simulation and design: using the BSIM-CMG standard*. Academic Press.
20. Bertrand, G., Deleonibus, S., Previtali, B., Guegan, G., Jehl, X., Sanquer, M., & Balestra, F. (2004). Towards the limits of conventional MOSFETs: case of sub 30 nm NMOS devices. *Solid-State Electronics*, 48(4), 505-509.
21. Saha, S. (1998). Effects of inversion layer quantization on channel profile engineering for nMOSFETs with 0.1 μm channel lengths. *Solid-State Electronics*, 42(11), 1985-1991.
22. Saha, S. K. (2001). U.S. Patent No. 6,323,520. Washington, DC: U.S. Patent and Trademark Office.
23. Saha, S. K. (1999, September). Drain profile engineering for MOSFET devices with channel lengths below 100 nm. In *Microelectronic Device Technology III* (Vol. 3881, pp. 195-204). SPIE.
24. Saha, S. K. (2002). U.S. Patent No. 6,344,405. Washington, DC: U.S. Patent and Trademark Office.
25. Saha, S. (2001). Scaling considerations for high performance 25 nm metal–oxide–semiconductor field effect transistors. *Journal of Vacuum Science*

& *Technology B: Microelectronics and Nanometer Structures Processing, Measurement, and Phenomena*, 19(6), 2240-2246.

26. Saha, S. (2001). Design considerations for 25 nm MOSFET devices. *Solid-State Electronics*, 45(10), 1851-1857.

27. Radosavljevic, M., Chu-Kung, B., Corcoran, S., Dewey, G., Hudait, M. K., Fastenau, J. M., ... & Chau, R. (2009, December). Advanced high-K gate dielectric for high-performance short-channel In 0.7 Ga 0.3 As quantum well field effect transistors on silicon substrate for low power logic applications. In *2009 IEEE International Electron Devices Meeting (IEDM)* (pp. 1-4). IEEE.

28. Caymax, M., Eneman, G., Bellenger, F., Merckling, C., Delabie, A., Wang, G., ... & Heyns, M. (2009, December). Germanium for advanced CMOS anno 2009: A SWOT analysis. In *2009 IEEE International Electron Devices Meeting (IEDM)* (pp. 1-4). IEEE.

29. Schwierz, F. (2010). Graphene transistors. *Nature Nanotechnology*, 5(7), 487-496.

30 Radisavljevic, B., Radenovic, A., Brivio, J., Giacometti, V., & Kis, A. (2011). Single-layer MoS2 transistors. *Nature Nanotechnology*, 6(3), 147-150.

31. Jeon, K., Loh, W. Y., Patel, P., Kang, C. Y., Oh, J., Bowonder, A., ... & Hu, C. (2010, June). Si tunnel transistors with a novel silicided source and 46mV/ dec swing. In *2010 Symposium on VLSI Technology* (pp. 121-122). IEEE.

32. Islam Khan, A., Bhowmik, D., Yu, P., Joo Kim, S., Pan, X., Ramesh, R., & Salahuddin, S. (2011). Experimental evidence of ferroelectric negative capacitance in nanoscale heterostructures. *Applied Physics Letters*, 99(11), 113501.

33. Radosavljevic, M., Dewey, G., Basu, D., Boardman, J., Chu-Kung, B., Fastenau, J. M., ... & Chau, R. (2011, December). Electrostatics improvement in 3-D tri-gate over ultra-thin body planar InGaAs quantum well field effect transistors with high-K gate dielectric and scaled gate-to-drain/gate-to-source separation. In *2011 International Electron Devices Meeting* (pp. 33-1). IEEE.

34. Tomioka, K., Yoshimura, M., & Fukui, T. (2012, June). Steep-slope tunnel field-effect transistors using III–V nanowire/Si heterojunction. In *2012 symposium on VLSI technology (VLSIT)* (pp. 47-48). IEEE.

35. Fujita, K., Torii, Y., Hori, M., Oh, J., Shifren, L., Ranade, P., ... & Ema, T. (2011, December). Advanced channel engineering achieving aggressive reduction of V T variation for ultra-low-power applications. In *2011 International Electron Devices Meeting* (pp. 32-3). IEEE.

36. Saha, S. (2016). U.S. Patent No. 9,299,702. Washington, DC: U.S. Patent and Trademark Office.

37. Saha, S. K. (2017). U.S. Patent No. 9,768,074. Washington, DC: U.S. Patent and Trademark Office.

38. Bohr, M. T., Chau, R. S., Ghani, T., & Mistry, K. (2007). The high-k solution. IEEE spectrum, 44(10), 29-35.

39. Subramanian, V., Kedzierski, J., Lindert, N., Tam, H., Su, Y., McHale, J., ... & Hu, C. (1999, June). A bulk-Si-compatible ultrathin-body SOI technology

for sub-100 nm MOSFETs. In *1999 57th Annual Device Research Conference Digest* (Cat. No. 99TH8393) (pp. 28-29). IEEE.

40. Balestra, F. (2013, June). Challenges and limits for very low energy computation. In *2012 IEEE 11th International Conference on Solid-State and Integrated Circuit Technology* (pp. 1-4). IEEE.

41. Cristoloveanu, S., & Balestra, F. (2009). Introduction to SOI technology and transistors. In *Physics and operation of Silicon devices and Integrated circuits*.

42. Choi, Y. K., Asano, K., Lindert, N., Subramanian, V., King, T. J., Bokor, J., & Hu, C. (1999, December). Ultra-thin body SOI MOSFET for deep-sub-tenth micron era. In *International Electron Devices Meeting 1999*. Technical Digest (Cat. No. 99CH36318) (pp. 919-921). IEEE.

43. Liu, Q., Yagishita, A., Loubet, N., Khakifirooz, A., Kulkarni, P., Yamamoto, T., ... & Sampson, R. (2010, June). Ultra-thin-body and BOX (UTBB) fully depleted (FD) device integration for 22nm node and beyond. In *2010 Symposium on VLSI Technology* (pp. 61-62). IEEE.

44. Yoo, D. W., & Joshi, Y. K. (2004). Energy efficient thermal management of electronic components using solid-liquid phase change materials. *IEEE Transactions on Device and Materials Reliability*, 4(4), 641-649.

45. Suzuki, E., Ishii, K., Kanemaru, S., Maeda, T., & Tsutsumi, T. Member IEEE, T. Sekigawa, K. Nagai, and H. Hiroshima 2000. *IEEE Trans. Electron Devices*, 47, 354.

46. Liu, Q., Vinet, M., Gimbert, J., Loubet, N., Wacquez, R., Grenouillet, L., ... & Sampson, R. (2013, December). High performance UTBB FDSOI devices featuring 20nm gate length for 14nm node and beyond. In *2013 IEEE International Electron Devices Meeting* (pp. 9-2). IEEE.

47. Barral, V., Poiroux, T., Andrieu, F., Buj-Dufournet, C., Faynot, O., Ernst, T., ... & Deleonibus, S. (2007, December). Strained FDSOI CMOS technology scalability down to 2.5 nm film thickness and 18nm gate length with a TiN/HfO 2 gate stack. In *2007 IEEE International Electron Devices Meeting* (pp. 61-64). IEEE.

48. Cheng, K., Khakifirooz, A., Kulkarni, P., Kanakasabapathy, S., Schmitz, S., Reznicek, A., ... & O'Neill, J. (2009, June). Fully depleted extremely thin SOI technology fabricated by a novel integration scheme featuring implant-free, zero-silicon-loss, and faceted raised source/drain. In *2009 Symposium on VLSI Technology* (pp. 212-213). IEEE.

49. Faynot, O., Andrieu, F., Weber, O., Fenouillet-Béranger, C., Perreau, P., Mazurier, J., ... & Deleonibus, S. (2010, December). Planar Fully depleted SOI technology: A Powerful architecture for the 20nm node and beyond. In *2010 International Electron Devices Meeting* (pp. 3-2). IEEE.

50. Wong, H. S., Frank, D. J., & Solomon, P. M. (1998, December). Device design considerations for double-gate, ground-plane, and single-gated ultra-thin SOI MOSFET's at the 25 nm channel length generation. In *International Electron Devices Meeting 1998*. Technical Digest (Cat. No. 98CH36217) (pp. 407-410). IEEE.

51. Suzuki, K., Tanaka, T., Tosaka, Y., Horie, H., & Arimoto, Y. (1993). Scaling theory for double-gate SOI MOSFET's. *IEEE Transactions on Electron Devices*, 40(12), 2326-2329.
52. Auth, C., Allen, C., Blattner, A., Bergstrom, D., Brazier, M., Bost, M., ... & Mistry, K. (2012, June). A 22nm high performance and low-power CMOS technology featuring fully-depleted tri-gate transistors, self-aligned contacts and high density MIM capacitors. In *2012 symposium on VLSI technology (VLSIT)* (pp. 131-132). IEEE.
53. Merritt, R. (2012). TSMC taps ARM's V8 on road to 16-nm FinFET. EE Times..
54. Hisamoto, D., Lee, W. C., Kedzierski, J., Takeuchi, H., Asano, K., Kuo, C., ... & Hu, C. (2000). FinFET-a self-aligned double-gate MOSFET scalable to 20 nm. *IEEE Transactions on Electron Devices*, 47(12), 2320-2325.
55. Natarajan, S., Agostinelli, M., Akbar, S., Bost, M., Bowonder, A., Chikarmane, V., ... & Zhang, K. (2014, December). A 14nm logic technology featuring 2 nd-generation finfet, air-gapped interconnects, self-aligned double patterning and a 0.0588 μm 2 sram cell size. In *2014 IEEE International Electron Devices Meeting* (pp. 3-7). IEEE.
56. James, D. (2012, September). Intel Ivy Bridge unveiled—The first commercial tri-gate, high-k, metal-gate CPU. In *Proceedings of the IEEE 2012 Custom Integrated Circuits Conference* (pp. 1-4). IEEE..
57. Kedzierski, J., Ieong, M., Nowak, E., Kanarsky, T. S., Zhang, Y., Roy, R., ... & Wong, H. S. (2003). Extension and source/drain design for high-performance FinFET devices. *IEEE Transactions on Electron Devices*, 50(4), 952-958.
58. Razavieh, A., Zeitzoff, P., & Nowak, E. J. (2019). Challenges and limitations of CMOS scaling for FinFET and beyond architectures. *IEEE Transactions on Nanotechnology*, 18, 999-1004.
59. Zheng, P., Connelly, D., Ding, F., & Liu, T. J. K. (2015). FinFET evolution toward stacked-nanowire FET for CMOS technology scaling. *IEEE Transactions on Electron Devices*, 62(12), 3945-3950.
60. Iwai, H., Natori, K., Kakushima, K., Ahmet, P., Oshiyama, A., Shiraishi, K., ... & Ohmori, K. (2010, September). Si nanowire device and its modeling. In *2010 International Conference on Simulation of Semiconductor Processes and Devices* (pp. 63-66). IEEE.
61. Ziegler, A., & Luisier, M. (2018). Complex Band Structure Effects in k.p-Based Quantum Transport Simulations of p-Type Silicon Nanowire Transistors. *IEEE Transactions on Electron Devices*, 65(4), 1298-1302.
62. Colinge, J. P., Lee, C. W., Afzalian, A., Akhavan, N. D., Yan, R., Ferain, I., ... & Murphy, R. (2010). Nanowire transistors without junctions. *Nature Nanotechnology*, 5(3), 225-229.
63. Bangsaruntip, S., Cohen, G. M., Majumdar, A., & Sleight, J. W. (2010). Universality of short-channel effects in undoped-body silicon nanowire MOSFETs. *IEEE Electron Device Letters*, 31(9), 903-905.

64. Takato, H., Sunouchi, K., Okabe, N., Nitayama, A., Hieda, K., Horiguchi, F., & Masuoka, F. (1991). Impact of surrounding gate transistor (SGT) for ultra-high-density LSI's. IEEE *Transactions on Electron Devices*, 38(3), 573-578.
65. Nitayama, A., Takato, H., Okabe, N., Sunouchi, K., Hieda, K., Horiguchi, F., & Masuoka, F. (1991). Multi-pillar surrounding gate transistor (M-SGT) for compact and high-speed circuits. IEEE *Transactions on Electron Devices*, 38(3), 579-583.
66. Watanabe, S., Tsuchida, K., Takashima, D., Oowaki, Y., Nitayama, A., Hieda, K., ... & Hara, H. (1995). A novel circuit technology with surrounding gate transistors (SGT's) for ultra high density DRAM's. *IEEE Journal of Solid-State Circuits*, 30(9), 960-971.
67. Colinge, J. P. (2004). Multiple-gate soi mosfets. *Solid-state Electronics*, 48(6), 897-905.
68. Yan, R. H., Ourmazd, A., & Lee, K. F. (1992). Scaling the Si MOSFET: From bulk to SOI to bulk. IEEE *Transactions on Electron Devices*, 39(7), 1704-1710.
69. Yakimets, D., Eneman, G., Schuddinck, P., Bao, T. H., Bardon, M. G., Raghavan, P., ... & De Meyer, K. (2015). Vertical GAAFETs for the ultimate CMOS scaling. IEEE *Transactions on Electron Devices*, 62(5), 1433-1439.
70. Yang, F. L., Lee, D. H., Chen, H. Y., Chang, C. Y., Liu, S. D., Huang, C. C., ... & Hu, C. (2004, June). 5nm-gate nanowire FinFET. In Digest of Technical Papers. *2004 Symposium on VLSI Technology*, 2004. (pp. 196-197). IEEE.
71. Singh, N., Lim, F. Y., Fang, W. W., Rustagi, S. C., Bera, L. K., Agarwal, A., ... & Kwong, D. L. (2006, December). Ultra-narrow silicon nanowire gate-all-around CMOS devices: Impact of diameter, channel-orientation and low temperature on device performance. In *2006 International Electron Devices Meeting* (pp. 1-4). IEEE.
72. Suk, S. D., Lee, S. Y., Kim, S. M., Yoon, E. J., Kim, M. S., Li, M., ... & Ryu, B. I. (2005, December). High performance 5nm radius Twin Silicon Nanowire MOSFET (TSNWFET): fabrication on bulk si wafer, characteristics, and reliability. In *IEEE International Electron Devices Meeting*, 2005. IEDM Technical Digest. (pp. 717-720). IEEE.
73. Yeo, K. H., Suk, S. D., Li, M., Yeoh, Y. Y., Cho, K. H., Hong, K. H., ... & Ryu, B. I. (2006, December). Gate-all-around (GAA) twin silicon nanowire MOSFET (TSNWFET) with 15 nm length gate and 4 nm radius nanowires. In *2006 International Electron Devices Meeting* (pp. 1-4). IEEE.
74. Singh, N., Lim, F. Y., Fang, W. W., Rustagi, S. C., Bera, L. K., Agarwal, A., ... & Kwong, D. L. (2006, December). Ultra-narrow silicon nanowire gate-all-around CMOS devices: Impact of diameter, channel-orientation and low temperature on device performance. In *2006 International Electron Devices Meeting* (pp. 1-4). IEEE.
75. Jiang, Y., Liow, T. Y., Singh, N., Tan, L. H., Lo, G. Q., Chan, D. S. H., & Kwong, D. L. (2008, June). Performance breakthrough in 8 nm gate length gate-all-around nanowire transistors using metallic nanowire contacts. In *2008 Symposium on VLSI Technology* (pp. 34-35). IEEE.

46. Tian, Y., Huang, R., Wang, Y., Zhuge, J., Wang, R., Liu, J., ... & Wang, Y. (2007, December). New self-aligned silicon nanowire transistors on bulk substrate fabricated by epi-free compatible CMOS technology: Process integration, experimental characterization of carrier transport and low frequency noise. In *2007 IEEE International Electron Devices Meeting* (pp. 895-898). IEEE.

77. Ishikawa, F., & Buyanova, I. (Eds.). (2017). *Novel compound semiconductor nanowires: materials, devices, and applications.* CRC Press.

78. Park, J. T., & Colinge, J. P. (2002). Multiple-gate SOI MOSFETs: device design guidelines. *IEEE Transactions on Electron Devices,* 49(12), 2222-2229.

79. Sun, X., Moroz, V., Damrongplasit, N., Shin, C., & Liu, T. J. K. (2011). Variation study of the planar ground-plane bulk MOSFET, SOI FinFET, and trigate bulk MOSFET designs. *IEEE Transactions on Electron Devices,* 58(10), 3294-3299.

80. Li, C., Zhuang, Y., & Han, R. (2011). Cylindrical surrounding-gate MOSFETs with electrically induced source/drain extension. *Microelectronics Journal,* 42(2), 341-346.

81. Lieber, C. M. (2011). Semiconductor nanowires: A platform for nanoscience and nanotechnology. *MRS Bulletin,* 36(12), 1052-1063.

82. Jena, B., Dash, S., & Mishra, G. P. (2016). Electrostatic performance improvement of dual material cylindrical gate MOSFET using work-function modulation technique. *Superlattices and Microstructures,* 97, 212-220.

83. Ramkrishna, B. S., Jena, B., Dash, S., & Mishra, G. P. (2017). Investigation of electrostatic performance for a conical surrounding gate MOSFET with linearly modulated work-function. *Superlattices and Microstructures,* 101, 152-159.

84. Kim, M., Ko, H., Kang, M., & Shin, H. (2017, June). Comparison of parasitic components between LFET and VFET using 3D TCAD. In *2017 Silicon Nanoelectronics Workshop (SNW)* (pp. 91-92). IEEE..

85. Pan, C., Raghavan, P., Yakimets, D., Debacker, P., Catthoor, F., Collaert, N., ... & Naeemi, A. (2015). Technology/system codesign and benchmarking for lateral and vertical GAA nanowire FETs at 5-nm technology node. *IEEE Transactions on Electron Devices,* 62(10), 3125-3132..

86. Kaushal, G., Jeong, H., Maheshwaram, S., Manhas, S. K., Dasgupta, S., & Jung, S. O. (2015). Low power SRAM design for 14 nm GAA Si-nanowire technology. *Microelectronics Journal,* 46(12), 1239-1247.

87. Chen, G., Li, M., Fan, J., Yang, Y., Zhang, H., & Huang, R. (2016, May). Multi-V T design of vertical channel nanowire FET for sub-10nm technology node. In *2016 IEEE International Nanoelectronics Conference (INEC)* (pp. 1-2). IEEE.

88. Chen, G., Li, M., Zhang, J., Yang, Y., & Huang, R. (2016, October). Source/drain architecture design of vertical channel nanowire FET for sub-10nm node. In *2016 13th IEEE International Conference on Solid-State and Integrated Circuit Technology (ICSICT)* (pp. 1008-1010). IEEE.

89. Goel, A., Rewari, S., Verma, S., & Gupta, R. S. (2019). Temperature-dependent gate-induced drain leakages assessment of dual-metal nanowire field-effect transistor—analytical model. *IEEE Transactions on Electron Devices*, 66(5), 2437-2445.
90. Mendiratta, N., Tripathi, S.L. & Chander, S. Analytical Model of Dopingless Asymmetrical Junctionless Double Gate MOSFET. *Silicon* (2022). https://doi.org/10.1007/s12633-022-01819-z.
91. Verma, S., Tripathi, S.L. Impact & Analysis of Inverted-T shaped Fin on the Performance parameters of 14-nm heterojunction FinFET. *Silicon* (2022). https://doi.org/10.1007/s12633-022-01708-5.

6

Gate All Around MOSFETs-
A Futuristic Approach

Ritu Yadav[1*] and Kiran Ahuja[2]

[1]ECE Department, IK Gujaral Punjab Technical University, Jalandhar, India
[2]ECE Department, DAVIET, Jalandhar, India

Abstract

In this chapter, the history of semiconductor technology and its continuous development processes such as recent MOSFET technologies, the significance of scaling in CMOS technology, challenges in scaling, futuristic scaling method (technology booster) the introduction of high-K, circuit design, and device modeling techniques are discussed. Considering all these challenges in the current scenario, this study was undertaken with the key focus on reducing the leakage current, improving the subthreshold slope, and developing immunity against the short channel effect by introducing the hetero di-electric oxide (combination of high-K (HfO_2 and TiO_2) and traditional SiO_2) in triple asymmetric metal gate by quantization approach. Advance multiple devices such as Gate-all-around can be effectively used to improve the performance of the device in terms of the chip design area, speed, and power by using work function engineering and dielectric engineering. The quantum effect on the gate-all-around device is also discussed in detail.

Keywords: Gate-all-around (GAA), Sub-threshold voltage (SV), DIBL, SCEs

6.1 Introduction

VLSI (very large-scale integration) is an advanced and emerging field in the semiconductor industry for circuit implantation, system-level design, and memory applications. In the current scenario, when the usage of electronics in the fields of automation, information technology, wireless, and

---

Corresponding author: raoritu14@gmail.com

Abhishek Kumar, Suman Lata Tripathi, and K. Srinivasa Rao (eds.) Machine Learning for VLSI Chip Design, (95–112) © 2023 Scrivener Publishing LLC

telecommunication has been increasing day by day, then it becomes necessary to evolve such a technology that can make semiconductor chips smaller and lighter in weight, energy-efficient, with larger data handling, faster response time, and capable of sustaining the resources. This can be achieved by applying VLSI design techniques using ultra-small sizes with high integration density and low power consumption with enhanced performance, which is possible by using nano-scale technology by introducing new materials.

6.1.1 Semiconductor Technology: History

Before the 21st century, electronics fabrication was dependent on vacuum-tube technology. The key point in semiconductor history was the introduction of MOSFET by Lilienfeld [1, 2] in 1930, which replaced the vacuum-tube based with novel compact dimension semiconductor transistor technology, as shown in Figure 6.1(a,b). The author claimed that the proposed device used copper-sulfide semiconductor material three-electrode structure. However, fabrication feasibility was not possible in working devices. This concept was famous for the field-effect transistor. The p-n junction in 1940 [3] was discovered by the Ohl's serendipitous, and later, in 1948, W. Shockley developed a p-n junction-based transistor [4].

When in 1948 Shockley discovered the first transistor (BJT), he set a milestone in solid-state electronics. Compared to vacuum-tube technology, the BJT was more reliable and less power-consuming, but the fabrication approach was complex. Therefore, even with the amazing capabilities, the feasibilities of this novel technology required miniaturization to reduce the cost of the elements. Further enhancement in the performance of the VLSI the computer industry developed a MOSFET. In 1950 the first electronics computer was introduced, which was based on vacuum-tube technology,

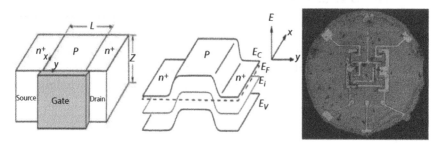

Figure 6.1 Traditional device structure of N-channel MOSFET and energy band. (b) First-IC fabricated by Jay Last [11].

and thereafter various inventions were also made by using this technology. The use of vacuum was weak and this technology became nonexistent because of complex circuit design. This device became the most popular in the electronics industry in the form of the rectifier and became a major component in the design of semiconductor devices. In 1951 Bell Laboratories [4, 5] successfully manufactured the first bipolar junction-based transistor. In 1958, Jack Kilby at Texas Instruments envisaged the thought of the (IC) and. Robert Noyce made the IC [6], as depicted in Figure 6.1(b). Richard Feynman in 1959 delivered a speech in which he said that the performance of the device may be enhanced by scaling down of devices. In 1959 Noyce developed a patent for the IC and with the help of this made multiple components on a single piece of silicon.

Two years later, in 1960, Atalla and Kahng constructed a MOSFET device based on silicon substrate by using SiO_2 as a dielectric [7], which was at that time widely used in the implantation of circuits design. Thereafter, the first commercial device was introduced by Texas Instruments and named 502 Binary Flip-Flop. In the following year, 1961, the "fully-integrated circuit" family was introduced [8].

After two years, the CMOS was invented [9, 10], which replaced the design structure from a few transistors with billions of transistors as shown in Figure 6.2. By Moore's law [12], transistors increase every year which enhances the packing density of transistors on a chip.

After that, in 1975, this concept was revised with the declaration that the number of transistors would be increased per year [13, 14]. This forecast is

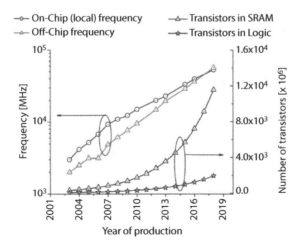

Figure 6.2 Increased numbers of transistors per year [17].

famously known as Moore's law and is applied as a ruling in the VLSI area. In 1971 the first microprocessor was developed by Ted Hoff and Stanley Mazor [15] and one of the popularly known ones was Intel's 4004.

The first commercial microprocessor enclosed 2300 transistors in a 16-pin IC of Intel, which introduced microprocessors accommodating above multi-billion transistors on a chip [1]. I.R. Committee [16, 17] presented the idea of scaling down devices by following the direction of the ITRS. However, this prediction had been implanted for three decades. Then transistor logic family [18] commenced the first microprocessor in 1972 which enclosed above two thousand pMOS transistors. As the growth of transistors increased exponentially according to Moore's law, other microprocessors were introduced based on nMOS technology but consumed more power due to the increased number of transistors per chip.

The latest technology required, like CPU can contain two billion transistors; however, CMOS technology is still the basic structural element of the circuitry for logic integrated circuits. Unfortunately, even the most innovative solution is CMOS technology which follows the scaling law. GPU processor-based Itanium-7quad contains 1.1 billion; this is possible with the help of scaling law. Scaling law defines shrinking the size of a device such that to acquire a smaller chip area while balancing the characteristics of MOSFETs.

6.2   Importance of Scaling in CMOS Technology

Downscaling of transistors improves the design structure of the device, improves the performance of the device, and reduces the cost. Dennard and fellow researchers in 1972 [19] proposed the scaling schemes. With the help of the same scaling factor, it can scale the device dimensions vertically and horizontally, hence it avoids the short channel effect (SCEs) and increases electrostatics controllability in the fabrication of smaller devices by the scaling factor. The main features of downscaling are the significant reduction in device dimensions, higher packing density, and dynamic power saving through lesser voltage, performance improvement and cost reduction.

In the latest scenario, with the help of scaling Itanium-7 quad-core GPU processor which contains 1.1 billion transistors and Intel 32nm static random access memory (SRAM) has about 800 billion transistors.

6.2.1   Scaling Rules

Leakage current is the major challenge in semiconductor CMOS technology. The literature survey reveals that shrinking the size of the gate length and oxide thickness decreased by scaling factor of 10^2, then biasing voltage reduced and packing density increased only by factor 10, power consumption increased by 10^5. The Semiconductor Industry Association (SIA) expects to achieve the 10 nm technology for the same various set of rules illustrated in Table 6.1.

Table 6.1 Scaling rule for MOSFET [21].

Microelectronics parameters	Scaling factor	Limiting factors	Resolution
Voltage Vdd	1/â	Thermal Voltage	Low operating temp.
Electric Field	I	-	-
Channel Length L	1/â	Lithography	Multiple gate structure follow gate engineering
Drain Current	1/â	Punch through	
Gate capacitance per unit area, Cox = εox/D	Â	Leakage current	Oxynitride
Gate area, Ag = L × W	1/â²		
Gate capacitance Cg = εoA/d	1/â		
Parasitic capacitance Cx	1/â		
Carrier density in channel, Q_{on} = Co Vgs Channel resistance R_{on} = 1/WQ$_{on}$	1 1	-	High mobility material/ strained devices/ Chemical process
Gate propagation delay Tpd	1/â	Non-Scalable Vdd	

(Continued)

Table 6.1 Scaling rule for MOSFET [21]. (*Continued*)

Microelectronics parameters	Scaling factor	Limiting factors	Resolution
Maximum operating frequency, fo	$\hat{a}^2$	Parasitic capacitance	Low K-insulator Copper wire
Saturation current, Idss	$1/\hat{a}$	Gate leakage current	Efficient power management High - k-dielectric
Current density, J	$\hat{A}$		
Switching energy per gate Eg = I Cg (VDD) 2/2	$1/\hat{a}^3$		
Power dissipation per gate, PgPg = Pgs + Pgd Both Pgs and Pgd are scaled by	$1/\hat{a}^2$		
Power speed product, PT = Pg Td	$1/\hat{a}^3$		
Transistor per chip	$\hat{a}^2$	Complexity in interconnection	Serial signal communication

The gate length thickness reduces by a scaling factor of $1/\hat{a}$, then operating voltage may be reduced by $1/\hat{a}$, and the circuit delay is reduced by $1/\hat{a}$. Consequently, there is degradation of the device characteristics and performance. So the forthcoming devices may be related to lower technology nodes [20]; have proposed finding alternatives to the consequences that occurred during downscaling of device size known as scaling rules for CMOS technology.

6.2.2 The End of Planar Scaling

The device miniaturizing happens through the process of scaling. The channel length is estimated to be 10 nm or below according to the 20 nm technology node [21]. The effect of scaling results in various SCEs such as degraded threshold-voltage, DIBL, subthreshold slope.

In the new millennium scaling came to an end because further, it was not possible to assure better electrostatic control of transistors, mainly because SCEs degraded the performance [22].

Short channels such as mobility degradation, named surface scattering, occurred by increasing the gate voltage in the channel region. Other effects are depletion capacitance and gate capacitance and these arose by increasing the EOT and therefore reducing the current of the device. The sub-threshold-swing should be closest to the ideal value (60mV/decade). Parasitic resistance effects were raised due to the down scaling of the channel length and the increased S/D (source to drain) resistances. Leakage current and GIDL (gate induced drain lowering) and hot-carrier effects arise due to ultra-scaling gate-oxide-thickness. Threshold voltage roll-off arises with scaling gate length. DIBL effects degraded the threshold voltage by increasing drain voltage. Continuous scaling of silicon-based substrate transistors provides better performance and reduces the thermal power budget. There is an emerging requirement, that demands continued scaling in various applications like data centers, memory banks, etc.

International Roadmap for Device and Systems (IRDS) predicted that after 2027 there will be no space for further downscaling of the device, because due to ultra-scaling some undesired issues arise in the device, such as gate tunneling, increasing the OFF current, and deteriorating the performance of the device.

6.2.3   Enhance Power Efficiency

Figure 6.3 illustrates the total power dissipation with respect to technology node.

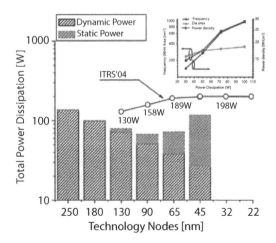

Figure 6.3 Total power dissipation with technology node [31].

This gap shows the requirement to control at the device level. The power requirement is estimated through equation 1.1 [23].

$$P_{dissipation} = P_D + P_S = \alpha\, fC_L V_{DD}^2 + V_{DD}\, (I_{Leakage} + I_{th}\, 10\, \frac{Vth}{ss})\quad (6.1)$$

In this equation P_D and P_S are the static and dynamic power dissipation, α is the scaling factor and C_L is the capacitance-load, V_{DD} is the drain-voltage which is lower than the power requirement is also lower, $I_{Leakage}$ and I_{th} are the total leakage current and threshold current, V_{th} is the minimum gate voltage if higher the threshold voltage lower the power consumption and SS is the subthreshold swing.

Some short channel effects such as gate tunneling scattering and quantum effect are provoked by reduction of gate oxide thickness, silicon thickness and doping concentration. To trade-off between power consumption and short channel effect (SCEs) the device required a substitute structure and architecture to keep on advanced CMOS scaling [24].

6.2.4   Scaling Challenges

Various types of scaling challenges are categorized mainly into two types, horizontal and vertical [25]. If shorter the Lg then degrades the threshold voltage, SCEs appeared under influence of higher drain voltage (Vds). In the ULSI (ultra-large-scale integration) industry gate length is represented by Lg, where L is the characteristic length defined in the equation

$$L_g = 0.1(X_j, t_{ox}, T^2_{dep})\quad (6.2)$$

These metrics such as oxide-thickness (tox), junction depletion width (Xj), and total depletion width (T2dep) must be vertically shrunk along with channel length (Lg) to reduce SCEs in bulk MOSFETs. There are the following effects because of vertical scaling in the device.

6.2.4.1   Poly Silicon Depletion Effect

Scaling of oxide leads to degradation of gate capacitance and transconductance and also increases the poly-deflection layer in the inversion mode. The deflection region cannot be reduced due to the limitation of doping (1019, 1020 cm-3). The result of this effect is in terms of shifting of the threshold voltage. This challenge can be avoided by using a metal gate.

6.2.4.2   Quantum Effect

Electric field increases near silicon/oxide interface due to downscaling of the oxide thickness. It creates quantum confinements of the carrier which lead to increased discrete sub-band and shifts the charge carrier from the interface.

6.2.4.3   Gate Tunneling

The use of the direct and Fowler Nordheim method of downscaling oxide thickness increased the static power dissipation. Employing high-k (HfO2 and Si3N4) reduces this effect.

6.2.5   Horizontal Scaling Challenges

In this lateral scaling, there is only scaling, of channel length (gate length) named as "Gate shrinking" which raised SCEs. There are the following horizontal scaling challenges.

6.2.5.1   Threshold Voltage Roll-Off

Threshold roll-off becomes extra impressive by the increased drain voltage. During scaling of channel length then depletion width becomes large than the channel length. Then channel barrier height reduces, which is manifested as threshold roll-off and DIBL.

6.2.5.2   Drain Induce Barrier Lowering (DIBL)

DIBL effects occur when source to channel barrier height is reduced by increasing the electrical field with high drain voltage. If there are decreases in the height of the barrier from source to channel then the carriers are without restraint inserted in the channel region. Therefore, the threshold voltage lower gate loses control over the channel. DIBL is also named the "charge sharing model". It is managed by the gate. The threshold voltage is calculated by the total depletion charge.

$$V_{th} = V_{fb} + 2\varphi - \frac{Qd}{cox} \qquad (6.3)$$

$$Q'd = Qd - \Delta Q \qquad (6.4)$$

Q'd, Qd, ΔQ are the depletion-charge in the gate region, total-depletion and depletion-charge in drain region V_{fb} flat-band voltage, V_{th} threshold voltage.

6.2.5.3   Trap Charge Carrier

The large electric field in the device produces a hot carrier (electrons) which has sufficiently high energy and momentum to inject the oxide and trap the Si/oxide interface; it causes the breaking of the Si-H band interface. Hot-carrier effects reduce the reliability of the device, increase the SCEs, decrease the V_{th} and increase the drive-current.

6.2.5.4   Mobility Degradation

Continuous miniaturization of the device requires more amount of channel doping concentration because it balances the electric field in the channel area. Higher doping concentrations avoid mobility scattering. Higher amount doping concentration creates dopant fluctuation inside the channel which results in mobility scattering and mobility roughness.

6.3   Remedies of Scaling Challenges

To overcome all these undesired SCEs, it is essential to increase the performance with novel technology boosters. Surface scattering can be enhanced by using various materials such as Germanium, Si-Ge or III-V compounds; these materials have better electron and hole mobility than silicon. Further, strain technology is most widely used to improve mobility.

By inserting high-k dielectrics gate capacitance is improved. Parasitic effects improved, OFF-current can be reduced by the implementing of silicon on insulator (SOI) layers, instead of bulk transistors.

However, even in multiple-gate MOSFETs, the reduced size of the device vertically and horizontally would be affected by SCEs [26, 27]. To reduce these effects, it is necessary to add together novel gate engineering and dielectric engineering [28–30] in the device structure.

6.3.1   By Channel Engineering (Horizontal)

By using the channel engineering technique in a multi-gate device structure the threshold-voltage increases and reduced SCEs in the device.

6.3.1.1   Shallow S/D Junction

This junction balances the space between the source and drain and maintained barrier height. In this way, the transport charge carrier movement from source to channel is less, compared to the deep shallow junction.

6.3.1.2   Multi-Material Gate

This is a very important method to reduce the hot-carrier effects. The multi-material gates combine gate architecture by two or more metals with dissimilar work function. The double and triple material gate were proposed by [32, 33] in 2008, which was based on the combination of two or three metal gates and with work-function in the source-side gate (M1) greater as compared to the drain-side gate (M2). This is due to the increased gate transport efficiency by increasing the electric field in the channel region [34] which reduces the hot-carrier effect in the dual metal gate (DMG) which is based on SOI MOSFETs.

6.3.2   By Gate Engineering (Vertical)

By employed gate-engineering in multi-gate structure [35], which is control the carrier by the gate in the channel region.

6.3.2.1   High-K Dielectric

To maintain EOT and continuous scaling the high-K was introduced by Intel in 2007 in 45nm CMOS technology. It replaces traditional oxide (SiO_2) with high–K (HFO_2 dielectric strength above 50).

6.3.2.2   Metal Gate

It improves the gate leakage problem in the CMOS technology gate stack employed by a combination of poly-Si/High-K. However, an experimental result shows mobility degradation by using a metal gate.

6.3.2.3   Multiple Gate

Fully depleted (FD) based on SOI MOSFET is a promising candidate to continue scaling; using this device enhances the transconductance, lowers Vth-roll-off and decreases the parasitic-capacitance, subthreshold-slope as compared to bulk MOSFETs. The incorporation of buried oxide (BOX) improves leakage current, and SCEs. However, using ultra scaling source/drain (S/D) region FD-MOSFET required high resistance, therefore to avoid the FIBL effects from the drain channel region it requires a special gate structure.

Various emerging devices are DG, triple-gate, FINFET gate, Quantum-wire, and FD-MOSFETs [36]. The circular, rectangular and quadruple gate-like gate-all-around [37], in FD-MOSFETs using buried oxide prevents encroachment EF lines in gate region which reduces the SCEs. But in this approach, it is not appropriate to increase the junction capacitance and body effects. The various gates such as double gate, the triple gate is the most promising device operated in enhancement and depletion mode. These devices are capable to face current challenges such as power consumption crises, control SCEs, and reduction of leakage current.

The GAA MOSFETs is one of the most potential candidates with better gate controllability and energy efficiency [38]. The gate-all-around offers characteristics length more scalability than double gate; the reason behind that gate covered all sides to channel and control transport carriers in the channel area. The device size below 25 nm provided the highest current drive capability due to current flow across the surface of the silicon body, so due to this reason ON –state drive mostly double than double gate device and strong confinement of electric field because the channel is surrounded by the gate. Switching characteristics and higher ON/OFF current ratio are better than traditional MOSFET. The subthreshold swing of GAA MOSFET is near to the ideal value at room temperature which enhances switching characteristics.

6.4 Role of High-K in CMOS Miniaturization

A high-K material having a dielectric constant greater than the SiO_2 is considered in the device design. The further miniaturization of microelectronic components is possible through the implementation of high-K strategy [39–41]. For the continuous process of downscaling of the transistor, the thickness of SiO_2 gate dielectric needs to be decreased.

However, decrease in SiO_2 thickness increases the capacitance and degrades the device performance. As ultra-scaling below 2-3 nm, leakage

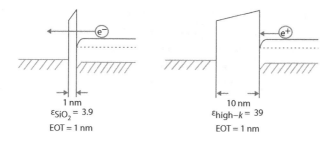

Figure 6.4 Effective oxide thickness (EOT) for high-K and conventional dielectric material [45].

current increases drastically, which is named "gate tunneling", which leads to increased static power and reduced reliability of the device [42, 43].

Keeping in view the leakage current, the device requires high-K dielectric along with SiO_2, so it is necessary to investigate the combination of high-K/TiO_2 material along with SiO_2 required for fabrication of the futuristic CMOS devices. Undoubtedly, Si-MOSFET with high-K may be the capable candidate for future generation devices, due to its higher dielectric constant than traditional SiO_2, as shown in Figure 6.4.

As per the prediction of Moore's Law, for continuing scaling of device advanced gate material is required instead of conventional dielectric material by following the main procedure for selecting substitute dielectric oxide are permittivity, di-electric strength, valence band offset, silicon process and crystal structure.

Other high-K materials [44] are Al_2O_3, HfO_2, TiO_2, La_2O_3, etc. But all of these materials are thermodynamically unstable, have high breakdown voltage, low defect density, low deposition temperature, and low charge states on silicon.

The combination of high-K/TiO_2 dielectric material along with SiO_2 must having more superior features in comparison to the high-K value [45].

A comparison has been made on the recently used high-K materials, i.e., SiO_2, HfO_2, $Al2O_3$ and TiO_2 in terms of structural and physical characteristics [46–51]. The high-K materials have better features in terms of the high-K, lower band-gap, and compatibility with silicon, so it is considered a potential candidate for MOS gate dielectric applications, as depicted in Table 6.2.

Table 6.2 Comparative analysis of traditional and high-K materials [46–51].

Di-electrical material	Di-electric strength (K)	Band-gap (Eg) (eV)	Conduction-band-offset ΔEc (eV)	Valence-band-offset ΔEv (eV)	Stability with Si	Crystal-structure
Silicon-dioxide ($Si\text{-}O_2$)	3.9	8.9	3.5	4.4	Yes	Amorphous
Aluminum oxide (Al_2O_3)	9.0	8.7	2.8	4.9	Yes	Amorphous
Hafnia oxide (HfO_2)	25	5.7	1.5	3.4	Yes	Monoclinic, cubic, tetragonal
Titanium oxide (TiO_2)	80	3.5	1.2	1.2	Yes	Tetragonal

6.5   Current Mosfet Technologies

The main challenges in recent semiconductor research are reduced power consumption, higher packing density, better scalability, balance leakage current, the large storage capacity of memories, and higher speed. The operational failures can be avoided by reducing the power consumption, which arises mainly due to the self-heating problem, which is fixed by the ITRS [52, 53]; further to enhance the performance of the devices the dimensions of the MOSFET are continuously decreasing. Following the novel device, such as the DG, the TG and the QGMOSFETs [54–57].

6.6   Conclusion

In this chapter, the key objective is to discuss a novel device based on nanoscale single and multi-asymmetrical hetero di-electric oxide gate-all-around nanowire for low power standby memory and sensor applications. This model is further suitable for circuit implementation. In this chapter the history of semiconductor technology and its continuous development processes such as recent MOSFET technologies, the significance of scaling in CMOS technology, challenges in scaling, futuristic scaling method (technology booster), introducing the high-K, circuit design, and device modeling techniques are discussed.

References

1. Intel; Intel Technology Road Map, http://www.intel.com accessed on 01/01/2020.
2. Lilienfeld, J. E., Method and Apparatus for Controlling Electric Currents. US Patent US1745175A. **1930**, New York, NY, USA.
3. Shaff, J. H. (**1947**). Development of Silicon Crystal Rectifiers for Microwave Radar Receivers. *Bell System Technical Journal*, **XXVI**(1), pp. 1-30.
4. Shockley. W (**1948**). Circuit Element Utilizing Semiconductor Material. US Patent US2681993A. New York, NY, USA.
5. Shockley, W. (1949). The Theory of P-N Junctions in Semiconductors and P-N Junction Transistors. *Bell System Technical Journal*. 28(3), pp. 435-489.
6. Kilby. J. S. (**1976**). Invention of the Integrated Circuit. *IEEE Transactions on Electron Devices*. 23(7), pp. 648–654.
7. Atalla, M. M. J., Kahng. D. (1963). Electric Field Controlled Semiconductor Device. U.S. Patent 3102230. New York, NY, USA.
8. Tsvedos, T.J. (1961). Introduction to Microsystems and the RCA Micromodule. *The RCA Micromodule Program: Components and Application,* AIEE Electronics Division, *Los Angeles, Symposium*, Los Angeles, California. pp. 3.
9. Wanlass F., Sah, C. (1963). Nanowatt Logic Using Field-Effect Metal-Oxide Semiconductor Triodes. In *Solid-State Circuits Conference. Digest of Technical Papers*. VI, pp. 32–33.
10. Wanlass, F. M. (1967). Low Stand-By Power Complementary Field Effect Circuitry. US Patent US3356858A. New York, NY, USA.
11. Last, J. (2020). First Planar Integrated Circuit Is Fabricated. https://computerhistory.org
12. Moore, G. (1975), Progress in Digital Integrated Electronics. In *Electron Devices*, 21, pp.11-13.
13. Moore, G. (1965). Cramming More Components on to Integrated Circuits. *Solid-State Electronics*. **38**, pp. 114-117.
14. Moore, G. (1929). *Understanding Moore's Law: The Future of Integrated Electronics*. Chemical Heritage Press. pp. 37-55.
15. Faggin, F., Hoff. J., M. E., Mazor, S. (1996). The History of the 4004. *IEEE Micro*.16(6), pp. 10–20.
16. I. R. Committee *et al.* (2007). International Technology Roadmap for Semiconductors.
17. International Technology Roadmap for Semiconductors, (SIA) (2003). http://public.itrs.net, SEMATECH, edition of ITRS.
18. Rabaey, J. M., (2003). *Digital Integrated Circuits*. Pearson Education Inc. 2nd edition, 07458.
19. Dennard, N. (1972). Design of Micron MOS Switching Devices. *IEDM Tech.* pp. 168-170.

20. Westlinder, J., Investigation of Novel Metal Gate and High–K Dielectric Material for CMOS Technologies. Doctoral Thesis, Department of Engineering Sciences, Uppsala University, SE-75105.
21. Skotnicki, T., Hutchby, J.A. (2005). The end of CMOS scaling toward the introduction of new materials and structural changes to improve MOSFET performance. *IEEE Dev.* 21 (1), pp. 16-26.
22. Chang, L., Choi, Y.C.Y. (2003). Extremely scaled silicon nano CMOS devices. *IEEE*, 91 (11), pp. 1860-1873.
23. Wang X. (2010). Simulation Study of Scaling Design Performance Characterization, Statistical Variability and Reliability of Decananometer MOSFETs. Doctoral Thesis, Department of Electronics and Electrical Engineering, University of Glasgow, G12 8QQ, Scotland.
24. Ferain, I., Colinge, C.A., Colinge, J. (2011). Multigate Transistor as the Future of Classical Metal Gate Oxide Semiconductor Field-Effect Transistors. *Nature*, 479, pp. 310-06.
25. Nowak, E.J. (2002). Maintaining the Benefit of CMOS Scaling When Scaling Bogs Down. *IBM Journal of R&D*, 46(2), pp. 169-180.
26. Gautam, R., Saxena, M. (2013). Gate All Around MOSFET with Vacuum Gate Dielectric for Improved Hot Carrier Reliability and RF Performance. *IEEE Trans Electron Dev.* 60(6), pp. 1820–1827.
27. Rahou, F. Z. (2016). Performance Improvement of Pi-Gate SOI MOSFET Transistor Using High-K Dielectric with Metal Gate. *IETE Journal.* 62(3), pp. 331-338.
28. Narula, V. (2019). Enhanced Performance of Double Gate Junctionless Field Effect Transistor by Employing Rectangular Core-Shell Architecture. *Semiconductor Science and Technology.* 34(10), pp. 1-11.
29. Zhang, J. W. (2014). Microstructure Optimization and Optical and Interfacial Properties Modulation of Sputtering-Derived Hfo2 Thin Films by Tio2 Incorporation. *Journal of alloys and Compounds.* 611, pp. 253-259.
30. Zhou, X., Long, W. (1998). A novel hetero-material gate (HMG) MOSFET for deep-submicron ULSI technology. *IEEE Trans. Elec. Device.* 45, pp. 2546-2548.
31. Mudge T. (2001). Power: A First-Class Architect Design Constraint. *IEEE Computer.* 34, pp. 52-58.
32. Long W. (1999). Dual Material Gate (DMG) Field Effect Transistors. *IEEE Trans. on Electron Devices*, 46(5), pp. 865-870.
33. Orouji, A. (2008). Nanoscale Triple Material Double Gate (TM-DG) MOSFET for Improving Short Channel Effects. *International Conference on Advances in Electronics and Micro-Electronics, Valencia, Spain, IEEE Proceedings.* pp. 11-14.
34. Jin, L. (2010). Two Dimensional Threshold Voltage Analytical Model of DMG Strained –Silicon on Insulator MOSFETS. *Journal of Semiconductors.* 31(8), pp. 084008(1-6).

35. Kumar M., Haldar S. (2014). Impact of Gate Material Engineering on Analog/ RF Performance of Nanowire Schottky Barrier Gate All Around MOSFET for Low Power Wireless Applications. *Microelectronics Journal.* 45(11), pp. 1508-14.

36. Tiwari P.K., Dubey S. (2010). A two-dimensional analytical model for threshold voltage of short-channel triple-material double-gate metal-oxide-semiconductor field-effect transistors. *J. Appl. Phys.* 108, 074508.

37. Fahad, H.M., Smith, C.E. (2011). Silicon Nanotube-Field-Effect Transistor with Core-Shell Gate Stacks for Enhanced High Performance Operation and Area Scaling Benefits. *Nano Lett.* 11 pp. 4393-4399.

38. Pratap Y., Ghosh P., Haldar S. (2014). An Analytical Subthreshold Current Modelling of Cylindrical Gate All Around (CGAA) MOSFET Incorporating the Influence of Device Design Engineering. *Microelectron Journal.* 45, pp. 408-415.

39. Gang, H., Deng B. (2013). Effect of Dimethyl Aluminium Hydride-Derived Aluminum Oxynitride Passivation Layer on the Interface Chemistry and Band Alignment of Hftio-Ingaas Gate Stacks. *APL Materials.* 1(1).

40. Chen, F. (2004). A Study of Mixtures of Hfo_2 and Tio_2 as High-K Gate Dilectrics. *Microelectron Eng.* 72, pp. 263-266.

41. Bera M.K., Maiti, C.K. (2006). Electrical Properties of Sio2/Tio2 High-K Gate Dielectric Stack. *Materials Science in Semiconductor.* 9, pp. 909-917.

42. Cho, K. (2002). First Principles Modeling of High–K Gate Dielectric Materials. *Computational Materials Science.* 23, pp. 43.

43. Chau, R. (2004). High-/Metal– Gate Stack Andits MOSFET Characteristics. *IEEE Electron Device Letter.* 25, pp. 408.

44. Chui, C.O. (2002). A sub 400° C Germanium MOSFET Technology with High-k Dielectric and Metal Gate. *IEDM Tech. Dig.* 8–11, pp. 437.

45. Iwai, H., Wong, H. (2006). On the Scaling Issues and High-K Replacement of Ultrathin Gate Dielectrics for Nanoscale MOS Transistors. *Microelectronics Engg.* 83, pp. 1867-1904.

46. Buchanan, D.A. (2000). 80nm Poly-Silicon Gated N-FETWith Ultra-Thin Al_2O_3 Gate Dielectrics for ULSI Applications. *IEDM Tech Digest.* pp. 223-226.

47. Perkins, C.M. (2002). Thermal Stability of Polycrystalline Silicon Electrodes on Zro_2. *Appl. Phys. Lett.* 81, pp. 1417-1419.

48. Dalapati, G.K. (2003). Electrical Properties of Ultrathin Tio2 Films on Si1-Ycy Hetero Layers. *Solid-State Electronics.* 47(10), pp. 1793–1798.

49. Gusev, E.P. (2003). Ultrathin Hfo2films Grown on Silicon by Atomic Layer Deposition for Advanced Gate Dielectrics Applications. *Microelectronic Engineering.* 69(24), pp. 145-151.

50. Choudhary, P. (2008). The Structural and Electrical Properties of Tio_2 Thin Films Prepared by Thermal Oxidation. *Condensed Matter.* 403(19), pp. 3718-3723.

51. 2012. International Technology Roadmap for Semiconductors (ITRS).

52. Arora, N. (2017). *MOSFET Models for VLSI Simulation.* WorldScientificPublishing.596224.

53. Iniguez, B. (2006). Compact-Modeling Solutions for Nanoscale Double-Gate and Gate-All-Around MOSFETs. *IEEE Transactions.* 53(9), pp. 2128–2142.

54. Colinge, J.P. (1990). Silicon-Insulator 'Gate-All-Around Device. *Electron Devices Meeting IEDM*, pp.595–598.

55. Colinge, J.P. (2007). Multiple-Gate SOI MOSFETS. *Solid-State Electronics.* 48, pp. 897–905.

56. Mendiratta, N., Tripathi, S.L. & Chander, S. Analytical Model of Dopingless Asymmetrical Junctionless Double Gate MOSFET. *Silicon* (2022). https://doi.org/10.1007/s12633-022-01819-z

57. Verma, S., Tripathi, S.L. Impact & Analysis of Inverted-T Shaped Fin on the Performance Parameters of 14-nm Heterojunction FinFET. *Silicon* (2022). https://doi.org/10.1007/s12633-022-01708-5

7

Investigation of Diabetic Retinopathy Level Based on Convolution Neural Network Using Fundus Images

K. Sasi Bhushan[1]*, U. Preethi[1], P. Naga Sai Navya[1], R. Abhilash[1], T. Pavan[1] and K. Girija Sravani[2]†

Department of Electronics and Communication Engineering, Lakireddy Bali Reddy College of Engineering (Autonomous), Mylavaram, Krishna District, AP, India
Department of Electronics and Communication Engineering, KL University, Green Fields, Vaddeswaram, Andhra Pradesh, India

Abstract

Diabetes is a complicated illness that requires immediate attention. While there is no cure for diabetes, learning to manage your medical condition, determining what will and will not improve your health, and doing everything you can to help yourself can significantly lessen the impact it has on your daily life. Diabetic retinopathy arises when diabetes damages the retina's small blood vessels. It can result in vision loss, "blind spots," and fuzziness. Your view may change from one day to the next, or even from dawn to sunset. This "fluctuating vision" can obstruct a variety of daily activities. Diabetic Retinopathy (DR) is a typical outcome of diabetes that results in vision misfortune or visual deficiency. Image estimation has become critical in modern medicine. Instruments are used to pinpoint the exact nature of a disease. As a result, we created a Convolution Neural Network–based computer model for predicting the severity of Diabetic Retinopathy (DR).

Keywords: Diabetic retinopathy, blood vessels, hemorrhages, fundus image, exudates, microneurysms, feature extraction, CNN

Corresponding author: sasibhushanlbrce123@gmail.com
†*Corresponding author*: kondavitee.sravani03@gmail.com

Abhishek Kumar, Suman Lata Tripathi, and K. Srinivasa Rao (eds.) Machine Learning for VLSI Chip Design, (113–126) © 2023 Scrivener Publishing LLC

7.1   Introduction

Around 250 BC, Apollonius of Memphis is supposed to have coined the term "diabetes." Diabetes was first mentioned in the medical literature in 1425, under the name diabete. In 1675, Thomas Willis coined the term "mellitus" to describe the condition. The reason for this was the sweet taste of pee. Diabetic retinopathy is a microvascular complication of diabetes that results in new-onset blindness in a significant proportion of patients. Eduard Jäger was the first to observe yellowish areas and whole or partial thickness extravasations through the retina in diabetic macular changes [1–4]. In 1872, Edward Nettleship published "Oedema or cystic infection of the retina," which included the main histological evidence of "cystoid degeneration of the macula" in diabetic patients, and Wilhelm Manz published "Proliferative adjustments in Diabetic Retinopathy," which included the meaning of tractional retinal separations and glassy discharge in diabetic patients. Arthur James Ballantyne's exploration, in any case, did not build up diabetic retinopathy as a novel sort of vascular illness until 1943. Various multi-focus clinical preliminaries have added incredibly to our comprehension of diabetic retinopathy's normal history in the course of the last ten years, setting up the worth of forceful glycaemic treatment in diminishing both the danger of advancement and the seriousness of the illness. In people aged 20 to 74, diabetic retinopathy is the significant reason for new instances of visual deficiency. Essentially all patients with type 1 diabetes and more than 60% of patients with type 2 diabetes [5–8] encourage retinopathy all through the first twenty years of their condition. As per the Wisconsin Epidemiologic Investigation of Diabetic Retinopathy (WESDR), 3.6% of more youthful sort 1 diabetes patients and 1.6% of more established sort 2 diabetes patients were legally visually impaired. Diabetic retinopathy was responsible for 86% of blindness in the younger-onset group. Diabetic retinopathy was responsible for 33% of the cases of legal blindness in the older-onset group, where other eye illnesses were common. Diabetic retinopathy is the leading cause of new incidents of blindness in those aged 20 to 74.

Diabetic retinopathy advances from gentle nonproliferative irregularities, which are set apart by expanded vascular penetrability, to direct and serious nonproliferative diabetic retinopathy (NPDR), which is set apart by vascular conclusion, to proliferative diabetic retinopathy (PDR), which is set apart by the arrangement of fresh blood vessels on the retina and back surface of the viterous. The retina and back surface of the glassy are portrayed by the arrangement of fresh blood vessels. Macular edema, which is characterized as retinal growing brought about by defective veins, can happen at any phase of retinopathy. These progressions can be sped up by pregnancy, adolescence, blood glucose control, hypertension, and waterfall medical procedure. In type 1 diabetic patients in their initial 3–5 years of diabetes or before adolescence, vision-undermining retinopathy is unprecedented. Virtually all sort 1 diabetes people gain retinopathy over the course of the following twenty years. At the hour of finding, up to 21% of individuals with type 2 diabetes have retinopathy, and the greater part foster some level of retinopathy over the long haul. Diabetic retinopathy can cause vision disaster inferable from a variety of components. Macular edema or thin nonperfusion can cause central vision impedance. PDR's new veins and tacky tissue withdrawal can bend the retina and cause tractional retinal partition, achieving extreme and all around irreversible visual adversity. Moreover, the fresh blood vessels may drain, expanding the danger of preretinal or glassy discharge. Finally, vision misfortune may be brought about by neovascular glaucoma connected with PDR.

Diabetes duration is likely the most important predictor of retinopathy development and progression. The regularity of any retinopathy was 8% at 3 years, 25% at 5 years, 60% at 10 years, and 80% at 15 years in the WESDR among more energetic starting diabetes patients. At 3 years, the prevalence of PDR was 0%, but by 15 years, it had risen to 25%. With the passage of time, the incidence of retinopathy increased as well. In the WESDR more youthful beginning gathering, the 4-year rate of creating proliferative retinopathy expanded from 0% in the first 5 years to 27.9% in quite a while, 13–14 years, of diabetes. The danger of acquiring PDR has stayed the same during the most recent 15 years.

7.2 The Proposed Methodology

The goal of diabetes medicine is to accurately predict diabetic issues and stop them from developing. Many of the studies in the literature are less reliable since they do not include picture pre-processing procedures. In this case, picture pre-processing is used to improve the image's features. The essential anatomical parts of the retinal vision are the macula, the optic circle, and the veins. A macula is a little region inside the retina of the eye where vision is the most clear. The film's macula is the light-touchy layer of retinal tissue. Blood traverses the body by means of veins, which are versatile cylinders or channels [9, 10].

Figure 7.1 Proposed method.

A component extraction part and an arrangement part are momentarily displayed in Figure 7.1 in our proposed technique.

As a directed learning calculation, CNN is applied for this situation. CNN is the best strategy for approximating any preparation information and further developing speculation on explicit datasets [11–13].

7.3   Dataset Description and Feature Extraction

7.3.1   Depiction of Datasets

EyePACS [15] made accessible a retinal dataset from the kaggle neighborhood area [14] that contains 88,702 significant standard retina pictures gathered under various settings of images. Each picture can be scaled from 0 to 4 levels of diabetic retinopathy in size.

7.3.2   Preprocessing

In our suggestion, enlarging the photographs [512x512] is an important step in the preprocessing. Before classification, the photos are converted to grey scale. From that point forward, the commotion is taken out from the changed fundus pictures utilizing the versatile middle channel. The middle channel is utilized to streamline the picture and lessen the bends brought about by the picture's good and bad limits [16, 17].

7.3.3   Detection of Blood Vessels

We have novel qualities for shading channels of communication (red, green, and blue) just as the normal of RGB esteems in our work, and the equation is yielded (7.1)

$$I = C_{red} \times R + C_{green} \times G + C_{blue} \times B \qquad (7.1)$$

Where I denotes the level of Intensity. Cred = 0.1, Cgreen = 0.7, and Cblue = 0.2 are colour channel coefficients extracted from a fundus image training set. The mask value is then determined in the same way as in (7.2).

$$mask\,(x,\,y) = \begin{cases} 1, & avg\,(R, G, B) < T_1, D < T_2 \\ 0 & otherwise \end{cases}$$
$$Where\ D = |R - G| + |R - B| + |G - B| \qquad (7.2)$$

The threshold values T1 and T2 are obtained by a trial and error approach. For the best results, T1 is set to 40 and T2 is set to 50. As in (7.3), the enhancement variable (S) is determined.

$$S = \frac{\sum_{i=1}^{n} \sum_{j=1}^{m} I\,(i,\,j)}{m \times n} \qquad (7.3)$$

The last expansion of the picture is finished utilizing the accompanying condition in (7.4) where I is the original picture of size (mxn).

$$C = \frac{(I - \min(I)e^s)}{\max(I) - \min(I)} \qquad (7.4)$$

The contrast improved image is C, the enhancement variable is S, and the processed image's minimum and maximum pixel values are (min, max).

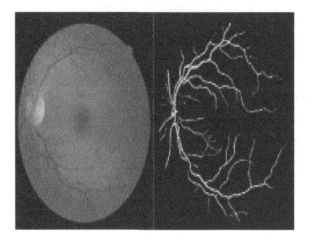

Figure 7.2 Detection of blood vessel.

Following normalisation, blood vessels become more visible against the background. A 2D Gaussian matching model's mathematical equation can be composed as (7.5).

$$G(x, y) = -\exp\left(\frac{x^2 + y^2}{2\sigma^2}\right) \qquad (7.5)$$

Where the standard deviation of the Gaussian operatoris σ and can be taken as the Gaussian filter's scale. Figure 7.2 displays the image's extracted blood vessels.

7.3.4   Microaneurysm Detection

Any place MAs have the best difference with the foundation in the recommended work, the green channel of the concealing complex body part picture has been used. Blood supply routes are reached out by dilatation, doubtlessly by topping off little openings and joining intermittent pixels. After applying the level plate shown in the being sorted out section SE (B) to the image A, the image is expanded (7.6).

$$A \oplus B = \{Z \,|\, (\hat{B}_Z \cap A) \uparrow \Phi\} \qquad (7.6)$$

Objects can be reduced using the Erosion operator after applying (7.6). By satisfying the (7.7), only the image's boundaries are engraved, leaving the rest of the image untouched.

$$A \ominus B = \left\{ Z \,|\, \left(B_Z \subseteq A \right) \right\} \qquad (7.7)$$

On the extended image of the retinal image, the erosion operator is utilised to totally remove the blood vessels. In most colour photos, capillaries are not apparent. Microaneurysms (MAs) appear to be detached from the retinal vascular network and are seen on capillaries [18, 19]. A Gaussian coordinating with channel is utilized to work on round dull patches. $I_{gauss} = I_{bothat}$ x gauss(1:0). The result response probability threshold is in (7.8).

$$I_{thresh} = thresh \left(I_{gauss}, 5\tau \right) \qquad (7.8)$$

The Threshold regard T is picked with the ultimate objective that the main 5% of pixels are picked. To deal with the kinds of the picked MA up-and-comers, a Fleming-based area progression development is embraced. Figure 7.3 portrays the recognition of microaneurysms in a picture.

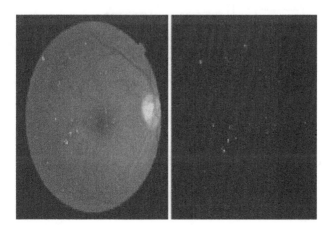

Figure 7.3 Detection of microaneurysm.

7.4   Results and Discussions

The CNN model is alluded to as the Resnet 152 model in this paper. All convolutional layers in ResNet models use the same convolutional window of size 3x3, and the number of filters grows as the depth of the networks climbs to 512. One max-pooling layer with a pooling size of 3x3 and a stride of 2 exists. In (7.9), the Convolution operation is illustrated.

$$(f*g)(t) \overset{def}{\approx} \int_{-\infty}^{\infty} f(\tau) g(t-\tau) d\tau \tag{7.9}$$

Figure 7.4 depicts the convolution neural network.

The essential objective is to diminish the expense of the Convolution Neural Networks (CNNs), which is reflected in the testing datasets. NoDR-0, MildDR-1, Moderate DR-2, Severe DR-3, and Proliferative DR-4 are the mathematically determined classifications in the organization.

The findings of CNN's categorization are depicted in the following diagrams see Figures 7.5–7.9.

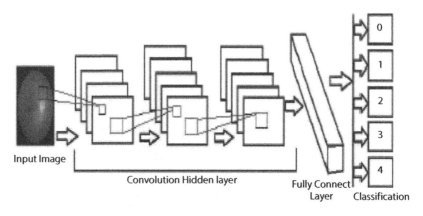

Figure 7.4 CNN architecture.

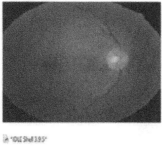

Result of

normal-DR

```
IDLE Shell 3.9.5                                                    —  □  ✕
File Edit Shell Debug Options Window Help
Python 3.9.5 (tags/v3.9.5:0a7dcbd, May  3 2021, 17:27:52) [MSC v.1928 64 bit (AMD64)] on win32
Type "help", "copyright", "credits" or "license()" for more information.
>>>
==== RESTART: C:\Users\UPPULURI PREETHI\Desktop\New folder\DR_SCALE\main.py ====
Imported packages
Model loaded Successfully
C:/Users/UPPULURI PREETHI/Desktop/New folder/DR_SCALE/sampleimages/images/eye1.png
Transforming your image...
Passing your image to the model....
Predicted Severity Value:  0
class is:  no dr
Predicted Label is 0
Predicted Class is no dr
```

Figure 7.5 Detection of normal–DR.

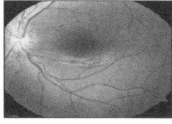

Result of

mild-DR

```
IDLE Shell 3.9.5                                                    —  □
File Edit Shell Debug Options Window Help
Python 3.9.5 (tags/v3.9.5:0a7dcbd, May  3 2021, 17:27:52) [MSC v.1928 64 bit (AMD64)] on win32
Type "help", "copyright", "credits" or "license()" for more information.
>>>
==== RESTART: C:\Users\UPPULURI PREETHI\Desktop\New folder\DR_SCALE\main.py ====
Imported packages
Model loaded Successfully
C:/Users/UPPULURI PREETHI/Desktop/New folder/DR_SCALE/sampleimages/images/eye3.jpg
Transforming your image...
Passing your image to the model....
Predicted Severity Value:  1
class is:  mild
Predicted Label is 1
Predicted Class is mild
```

Figure 7.6 Detection of mild–DR.

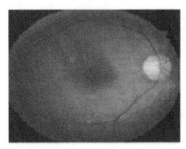

Result of

moderate-DR

```
|A| *IDLE Shell 3.9.5*                                                    —    □
File  Edit  Shell  Debug  Options  Window  Help
Python 3.9.5 (tags/v3.9.5:0a7dcbd, May  3 2021, 17:27:52) [MSC v.1928 64 bit (AMD64)]
n win32
Type "help", "copyright", "credits" or "license()" for more information.
>>>
==== RESTART: C:\Users\UPPULURI PREETHI\Desktop\New folder\DR_SCALE\main.py ====
Imported packages
Model loaded Successfully
C:/Users/UPPULURI PREETHI/Desktop/New folder/DR_SCALE/sampleimages/images/eye20.png
Transforming your image...
Passing your image to the model....
Predicted Severity Value:  2
class is:  Moderate
Predicted Label is 2
Predicted Class is Moderate
```

Figure 7.7 Detection of moderate–DR.

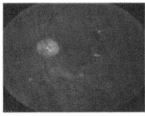

Result of

severe-DR

```
|A| *IDLE Shell 3.9.5*                                                    —    □
File  Edit  Shell  Debug  Options  Window  Help
Python 3.9.5 (tags/v3.9.5:0a7dcbd, May  3 2021, 17:27:52) [MSC v.1928 64 bit (AMD64)]  or
n32
Type "help", "copyright", "credits" or "license()" for more information.
>>>
==== RESTART: C:\Users\UPPULURI PREETHI\Desktop\New folder\DR_SCALE\main.py ====
Imported packages
Model loaded Successfully
C:/Users/UPPULURI PREETHI/Desktop/New folder/DR_SCALE/sampleimages/images/eye7.jpg
Transforming your image...
Passing your image to the model....
Predicted Severity Value:  3
class is:  severe
Predicted Label is 3
Predicted Class is severe
```

Figure 7.8 Detection of severe–DR.

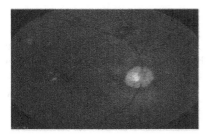

Result of

proliferative-DR

```
File  Edit  Shell  Debug  Options  Window  Help
Python 3.9.5 (tags/v3.9.5:0a7dcbd, May  3 2021, 17:27:52) [MSC v.1928 64 bit (AMD64)
] on win32
Type "help", "copyright", "credits" or "license()" for more information.
>>>
==== RESTART: C:\Users\UPPULURI PREETHI\Desktop\New folder\DR_SCALE\main.py ====
Imported packages
Model loaded Successfully
C:/Users/UPPULURI PREETHI/Desktop/New folder/DR_SCALE/sampleimages/images/eye9.jpg
Transforming your image...
Passing your image to the model....
Predicted Severity Value:  4
class is:  prolifrative
Predicted Label is 4
Predicted Class is prolifrative
```

Figure 7.9 Detection of proliferative–DR.

7.5   Conclusions

In this chapter, we have reported the Diabetic Retinopathy Level based on Convolution Neural network using fundus images. If the diabetic retinopathy is identified early on, it can help patients recover more quickly. The diagnostic procedure at the clinical stage is time-consuming and costly. Medical pictures processed using computer vision and rapid processing capacity might more accurately forecast illness. A computer model for predicting Diabetic Retinopathy (DR) levels is effectively constructed in this work. To further develop execution, the significant focal point of our investigation is on preprocessing and highlight extraction. Later on, we would prefer to assess the results of other profound learning models on other datasets to see which one performs better.

References

1. P. Zimmet and K. Alberti, "Diabetic mellitus and its complications: Definition, diagnosis, and classification. Section 1: Diabetic mellitus conclusion and classification." *Diabetic Medicine*, **1998**, Vol. 15, no. 7, pp. 539-553.
2. T.J. Lyons, M. Chen, T.M. Curtis, A. Jenkins, G.J. Mckay, T.A. Gardiner, A.W. Stitt, H.-P. Hammes, R.J. Medina, N. Lios, and R. Semo, "Diabetic

retinopathy: Advances in Understanding and Treatment" 2016, Vol. 51, pp. 156-186.

3. M.R.K. Mookiah, U.R. Acharya, C.K. Chua, C.M. Lim, E. Ng, and A. Laude., "Computer-aided diagnosis of diabetic retinopathy: A review," *Computers in Biology and Medicine* **2013**, Vol. 43, no. 12, pp. 2136-2155.

4. S.L. Rogers, R. Kawasaki, J.W.Y. Yau, and E.L. Lamoureux. "Worldwide Prevalence and Major Risk Factors of Diabetic Retinopathy," *Diabetic Care*, **2012**, vol. 35, pp. 556-564.

5. M. AI-Rawi and H. Karajeh, "A hereditary calculation with coordinating with channel streamlining for robotized distinguishing proof of veins from digitized retinal pictures," *PC Methods and Programs in Biomedicine*, **2007**. vol. 87, pp. 248-253.

6. S. Luo and L. Xu, "A Novel method for vein distinguishing proof from retinal pictures." *Biomedical Engineering Online*, **2010**, vol. 9, no. 1, p. 14.

7. H. Mi and K. Xu, D. Feng, "Profound Convolutional Neural Network-Based Early Automated Diabetic Retinopathy Detection Using Fundus Images", in Molecules, **2017**, vol. 22, no. 12, p. 2054.

8. A. Kori, S.S. Chennamsetty, M. Safwan K.P., V. Alex, "Ensemble of Convolutional Neural Networks for Automatic Grading of Diabetic Retinopathy and Mascular Edema." **2018**, arXiv: 1809.04228.

9. Q.Abbas., "Glaucoma-Deep: Detection of Glaucoma Eye Disease on Retinal Fundus Images Using Deep Learning." **2017**, *Worldwide Journal of Advanced Computer Science and Applications*, vol. 8, no. 6, pp. 98-106.

10. M.M. Hassan and S.M. Saiful, "Significant Learning-based Early Detection and Grading of Diabetic Retinopathy Using Retinal Fundus Images," **2018**, arXiv:1812.10595.

11. A.G. Casswell, F.R. Cophth, L.G. Ripley, G.L. Ong, R.S. Newsom M, "Fundus photography and a mechanized concealing differentiation edge test are utilized to survey for sight-undermining diabetic retinopathy," *American Journal of Ophthalmology*, **2004**, Vol. 6, pp-45-53.

12. Kumar, A., "Diabetic visual deficiency in India: The Emerging Situation," *Indian Journal of Ophthalmology*, **1998**, Vol. 23, pp. 245-252.

13. "Location of Diabetic Retinopathy," says Kaggle. [Accessed: October 1, **2019**]. [Online].

14. G. Bresnick and J. Cuadros, "EyePACS: An Adaptable Telemedicine System for Diabetic Retinopathy Screening," **2009**, *SAGE Journals* 14, 98-102.

15. S. Chatterjee, M. Nelson, S. Chaudhuri, N. Katz, "Using two-dimensional coordination with channels, veins in retinal images may be identified." **1989**, *IEEE Transactions on Medical Imaging*, 1989, Vol. 13, pp. 67-78.

16. V. Kouznetsova, M. Goldbaum, A. Hoover, "Piecewise limit assessing of a vein detection system developed using channel response in retinal pictures." In *IEEE Transactions on Medical Imaging*, **2000**, Vol. 19, no. 3, pp.56-65.

17. T. Walter, A. Erginay, P.Massin, C. Jeulin, R. Ordonezand, J.-C. Klein., *IEEE Transactions on Medical Imagaing*, **2011**, Vol. 12, pp. 987-998.

18. "Automatic identification of microaneurysms in colour fundus images," *Medical Image Analysis*, **2007**, Vol. 11, no. 6, pp. 555-566.
19. Prakash K.B., Sreedevi C., Lanke P., Vadla P.K., Ranganayakulu S.V., Tripathi S.L., Flower Detection Using Advanced Deep Learning Techniques. In Saini H.S., Singh R.K., Tariq Beg M., Mulaveesala R., Mahmood M.R. (eds.) *Innovations in Electronics and Communication Engineering. Lecture Notes in Networks and Systems*, Vol. 355, 2022, Springer, Singapore. https://doi.org/10.1007/978-981-16-8512-5_23

8

Anti-Theft Technology of Museum Cultural Relics Using RFID Technology

**B. Ramesh Reddy[1], K. Bhargav Manikanta[1], P.V.V.N.S. Jaya Sai[1],
R. Mohan Chandra[1], M. Greeshma Vyas[1] and K. Girija Sravani[2]***

*[1]Department of Electronics and Communication Engineering,
LBR College of Engineering, Mylavaram, Krishna District, Andhra Pradesh, India
[2]Department of Electronics and Communication Engineering, KL University,
Green Field, Vaddeswaram, Guntur, Andhra Pradesh, India*

Abstract

As progress progressed, the galleries showed a growing number of social relics, the number of visitors expanded, and definitely, valuable exhibits were taken by an expanding number of hoodlums. Customary techniques to prevent robbery cannot stop them. This examination gives a gallery a hostile to burglary strategy dependent on RFID innovation, which utilizes uninvolved RFID perusers/journalists to evaluate whether social resources are inside the protected reach. The RFID labels are attached to the social fortunes, and when they are taken out, they leave the powerful RFID ID range, alarming the framework and setting off the counter-burglary system. The suggested against robbery strategy checking is more prompt and has a higher security factor, and it is anything but restricted by the constraints of a customary infrared enemy of burglary, entryway attractive discovery, and different strategies. At long last, this exertion involves equipment circuit plans, programming advancement, and a progression of testing to get the necessary outcomes.

Keywords: RFID, reader, RFID tag

*Corresponding author: kondavitee.sravani03@gmail.com

Abhishek Kumar, Suman Lata Tripathi, and K. Srinivasa Rao (eds.) Machine Learning for VLSI
Chip Design, (127–138) © 2023 Scrivener Publishing LLC

8.1   Introduction

As individuals' social life has improved, craftsmanship displays and galleries have become a major attraction for explorers from one side of the planet to the other. By the start of 2019, China's total number of galleries had risen to 5,136. Exhibition halls have consistently viewed not-for-profits and public advantage as a social accord. Numerous administrations command that historical centers be free to general society. In 2018, the National Museum introduced more than 20,000 shows, drawing in around 1 billion guests and urging individuals to make a habit of visiting historical centers. Subsequently, the historical centers social fortunes have attracted greater levels of criminality. Burglary of curios is something that nobody likes to see. The historical center will plan the scope of social relics security strategies to guarantee the exhibition hall's wellbeing. In any case, burglary is boundless even in this climate.

The criminal alert is the most broadly utilized enemy of burglary innovation, with applications in a wide scope of businesses. Against-burglary alert frameworks introduced in monetary establishments, like banks, ATMs, and different areas can help to lessen the number of burglaries. Hostile-to-burglary frameworks can recognize gatecrashers, yet the main part of data in military areas should remain classified. In high-traffic regions, for example, train stations and schools, face acknowledgment innovation might be utilized to advise guilty parties and suspected individuals on the boycott. This fruitful strategy can limit the quantity of savage and criminal occurrences to secure individuals' lives and property, and thief caution gadgets are broadly used locally to ensure inhabitants' property and are transferred to the police as evidence. But every system has its limitations where there are situations they can network. So to overcome these problems our paper mainly focuses on Radio Frequency Identification Technology.

8.2   Literature Survey

The Internet of Things is an example of rapidly growing technology in the modern world and new technologies are emerging day by day with improving functionalities. The basic idea behind this spreading technology like RFID sensors, actuators, is to create an intercommunication channel between those technologies. This technology plays an important role in both working and domestic fields. Some of the technologies developed for domestic fields are e-health, enhanced learning, etc., and on the working field the technologies such as transportation, automation, industrial management, etc. [1].

The suggestion of Radio Frequency Identification innovation expresses that there are a few different ways of execution to ensure the things and trimmings in arcades or galleries, yet every one of the advances has its limits. A portion of the model is a glass breaking locator which demonstrates the sign if and just if the sensor is in the scope of following the sound, this is the constraint of glass breaking identifier. Here the authors S.B.A. Hamid, A.D. Rosli, W. Ismail, and A-Z. Rosli address the idea of RFID innovation for following the exhibition hall things in Turkey. This idea is made by knowing what RFID can do [2].

RFID (Radio Frequency Identification) is an information stockpiling and recovery strategy that gives remarkable IDs to things. It accompanies both an RFID peruser and an RFID tag. An RFID peruser is a gadget that communicates radio waves and gets signals from RFID labels and has at least one receiving wire. The RFID Tag has an interesting ID number that contains all data about the predetermined article. The Anti-burglary System comprises an RFID peruser, an RFID tag, and an interface gadget. After interfacing the Tag with the chosen object, it is anything but an alarm sign to the RFID peruser gadget [3].

The R. Tesorieo provides a system that is connected to both active and passive RFID and may be evaluated at art museums using mobile devices. The individual benefited from this concept since he could access necessary information without having to physically look for it [4].

The creator Geeth Jitendra presents a method of securing social resources by using a vehicle immobilizer, which has the advantage of being impervious to programmer assaults. A sending unit, a getting unit, and a keen vehicle interface make up the fundamental structure of the immobilizing framework. The information received will be placed in the vehicle, while the transmitter will be kept with the proprietor, ensuring that the transmitter and beneficiary have a functioning correspondence channel until they are within 200 meters of one another. As a result of its high pace of insurance against hacking assaults, this framework beats other systems. Others are powerless against digital assaults [5–12].

8.3   Software Implementation

The Arduino is programmed in such a way that it can communicate with the RFID reader, IR Sensor, Temperature Sensor. Arduino is flexible; it can be used to program in different languages. They all communicate with each other by sending the radio signal from the transceiver of the RFID reader through the antenna, and when the RFID tags come in the range of the radio signal, the tag uses this signal as a power to activate the Transponder in the microchip of RFID tags. This RFID tag sends the information about the cultural relic just like a unique id to the Tx present in the RFID reader. So this information can be accessed by the computer whenever needed.

8.4   Components

8.4.1   Arduino UNO

The Arduino Uno is a well-known open-source microcontroller board based on the Microchip ATmega328P microcontroller. Arduino.cc created the Arduino Uno. The board is entirely composed of analog and digital pins, which are then assigned to input or output pins. These digital and analog pins can then be connected to a variety of electronic devices, boards, and circuits. The Arduino Uno has 14 digital I/O pins as well as 6 analog I/O pins (Figure 8.1).

8.4.2   EM18 Reader Module

The EM18 Reader Module is a Radio Frequency Identification (RFID) Reader that is utilized to peruse RFID labels with frequencies of 125 kHz. The EM18 module reads the RFID labels and sends the remarkable ID to the PC or microcontroller utilizing diverse correspondence methods like UART and so forth. It peruses the information which contains an ID which is 12 bytes. It is not difficult to utilize and of minimal expense, low force utilization. The interfacing is finished with Microcontrollers utilizing UART and with PC utilizing RS232 convertor (Figure 8.2).

Figure 8.1 The top view of the Arduino UNO

Figure 8.2 The topview EM18 reader modules.

8.4.3   RFID Tag

The RFID tags are used to identify the objects, persons, etc. It contains the unique ID to identify the object and it senses the presence of the object in the museum in this project. The RFID tag has a frequency of 125KHZ and contains a 32 bit unique ID (Figure 8.3).

8.4.4   LCD Display

The LCD used here is a 16x2 display which is a yellow and green backlight ASCII Alphanumeric Character Display. 16x2 display means 16 characters by 2-line display. It has 16 pins and can operate in 4-bit mode with only four data lines or 8-bit mode with all eight data lines (Figure 8.4).

Figure 8.3 The proposed RFID tag.

Figure 8.4 The measurment LCD display.

8.4.5   Sensors

8.4.5.1   Fire Sensor

Fire sensors are utilized in autos, clinical gadgets, PCs, cooking apparatuses, and different sorts of hardware. They measure the temperature of an item or climate where it is available by coming into contact with the article or by identifying infrared energy transmitted by the item just as the environmental factors (Figure 8.5).

8.4.5.2   IR Sensor

Infrared radiation was discovered in 1800 by cosmologist William Herchel. It is a piece of electronic gear that actions and identifies infrared radiation in its current circumstance. Infrared sensors are characterized into two sorts: dynamic and aloof. Detached sensors recognize infrared radiation

Figure 8.5 The proposed fire sensor.

Figure 8.6 The proposed IR sensor.

but do not discharge it, so they are utilized in this task. These sensors are normally utilized in moving-based location applications. At the point when a moving article producing infrared radiation enters the detecting scope of the finder, the distinction in IR levels between the two pyro-electric components is estimated. The sensor then, at that point, speaks with the PC through an electronic sign (Figure 8.6).

8.4.6 Relay

A relay is an electrically controlled switch. It is made up of a set of input terminals for single or multiple control signals, as well as a set of operating contacting terminals. It works on the principle of electromagnetic

Figure 8.7 The proposed relay.

induction. Relays control one electrical circuit by opening and closing contacts with another electrical circuit (Figure 8.7).

8.5 Working Principle

The above block diagram shows the proposed model of our project. The model consists of Arduino UNO, EM-18 Reader Module, RFID Tag, LCD, Relay as its major components. A few sensors like fire Sensors, IR sensors are connected for the additional requirement.

8.5.1 Working Principle

The principal equipment segments incorporate Arduino, Radio Frequency Identification, LCD, Infrared, and temperature Sensors. The data from the framework is gotten by Arduino. What's more, it is customized in such a way. Radio Frequency Identification is an information stockpiling and recovery innovation that gives a personality code to screen objects. By and large, it is comprised of an RFID peruser, a radio wire, and an RFID tag. The unmistakably recognizable proof code is saved in the information base as a personality code. While, contingent upon the particular article, other data about the checked item is additionally put away on the RFID tag.

To screen and control the RFID per user information, a comparing application is introduced on the PC. The electronic tag is versatile and can be introduced on a surface without endangering the fundamental attributes or capacity of the curio. It speaks with the RFID scanner through

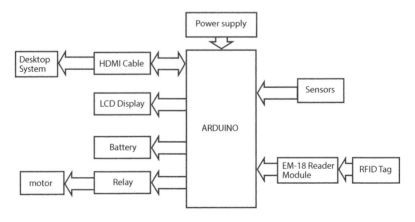

Figure 8.8 Block diagram of the proposed system.

remote innovation. The perusing scope of an RFID peruser can be sensibly stretched out according to the force size and application program. At standard stretches, the data from each electronic tag is perused to decide if the electronic tag is inside the reach (Figure 8.8).

An RFID peruser's two principal parts are a regulator unit and a radio recurrence handset module. RFID labels are made out of a chip and a coupling component, and each tag has an extraordinary code that is appended to the outside of the object and can be distinguished. The tag has two memory regions, one for putting away the ID and the other for putting away client data information, which can be changed and erased.

8.6   Results and Discussions

To obtain the desired output, all of the components are connected in this manner. Dumping the codes into the respective Arduino, which will then perform their operations and communicate with one another. We use Assembly language to dump code into Arduino.

This Image shows the RFID tag on the RFID reader module, which detects the card in the range or not. When the RFID tag in the range the blue led will glow and shows the safe message on the LCD screen as shown in Figure 8.9(a).

When the Tag is not in the range the blue led will be in OFF condition and it does not show in the LCD as shown in Figure 8.9(b).

Figure 8.9 The measurment results.

(a)

Figure 8.9(a) The measurment results.

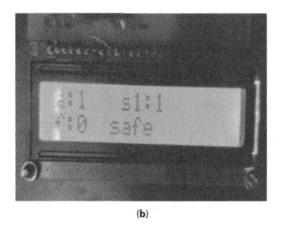

(b)

Figure 8.9(b) The measurment results.

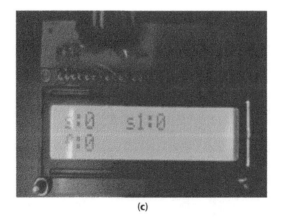

(c)

Figure 8.9(c) The measurment results.

(d)

Figure 8.9(d) The measurment results.

Here we declare the two Infrared sensors as's' and 's1'. When the object is in the IR range it shows '0' in the display and when the object is not in the range it shows '1' in the display as shown in Figure 8.9(c).

Here we declared the fire sensor as 'F'. When fire or smoke is not detected it shows '0' in the display and when the fire is detected the message 'fire detected' as shown in Figure 8.9(d).

8.7   Conclusions

This chapter proposes an alternative way to deal with galleries hostile to robbery plans dependent on the Internet of Things (IoT) innovation, which decides if social relics are inside range utilizing Passive Radio Frequency Identification perusers or journalists. On the off chance that an interloper moves toward the item and endeavors to burglarize it, the RFID tag and RFID peruser will impart, and the signal will sound, and information will be transferred to the IoT stage.

So by using this technology we can reduce thefts in a museum by identifying the abnormal in the RF field. In an existing system, we have an Infrared based security system to identify the theft.

So this technology was further extended by adding GPS Module to the object and to track the location of the object. So if the thief breaks all the above-mentioned safety measures and steals the object he or she can be found by tracking the location using the GPS Module.

References

1. N.- A. Çayirezmez, H.- M. Aygün and L. Boz, "Idea of RFID innovation for following exhibition hall objects in Turkey", *Proc. Computerized Heritage Int. Congr.* **2013**, pp. 315-318.
2. S. B. A. Hamid, A.- D. Rosli, W. Ismail, and A. Z. Rosli, "Plan and execution of RFID-based enemy of robbery framework", *Proc. IEEE Int. Conf. Control Syst. Comput. Eng.* (ICCSCE), 2012, pp. 452-457.
3. V. Lakafosis, A. Rida, R. Vyas, L. Yang, S. Nikolaou and M. M. Tentzeris, "Progress towards the principal remote sensor organizations of based RFID-empowered sensor labels", *Proc. IEEE*, 2010, Vol. 98, no. 9, pp. 1601-1609.
4. Z. Meng and Z. Li, "RFID tag as a sensor—A survey on the imaginative plans and applications", *Meas. Sci. Fire Up.*, vol. 16, no. 6, pp. 305-315, Dec. 2016.
5. E. Valero, A. Adán and C. Cerrada, "Advancement of RFID applications in development: A writing survey", *Sensors Journal*, 2015, Vol. 15, no. 7, pp. 15988-16008.
6. F. Sahba, "Historical center computerization with RFID", *Proc. World Automat. Congr.* (WAC), 2014, pp. 19-22.
7. X. B. Yang, "On the counter robbery innovation of present day exhibition halls", *Mod. Phys.*, vol. 23, no. 5, pp. 43-46, Oct. 2011.
8. Y. C. Shen and S. Q. Shen, "Radiofrequency recognizable proof innovation and its improvement status", *Electron. Technol. Appl.* 1999, Vol. 1, pp. 2-3.
9. J. Shi, "Imaginative use of significant distance RFID in the security field", *China Public Saf.* (Complete Ed.), 2006, Vol. 5, pp. 71-74.
10. Z. G. Feng, "Analysis of the theory of wisdom museum", *Museum Res.* 2019, Vol. 1, pp. 19-25.
11. W. Xiaohua, "Exploration on enemy of robbery issue in RFID library", *China Electron. Trade* (RFID Technol. Appl.), 2009, Vol. 4, no. 3, pp. 35-37.
12. X. Liu, B. Xiao, K. Li, X. Liu, J. Wu, X. Xie, *et al.*, "RFID assessment with blocker labels", *IEEE/ACM Trans. Netw.* 2017, Vol. 25, no. 1, pp. 224-237.

9

Smart Irrigation System Using Machine Learning Techniques

B. V. Anil Sai Kumar, Suryavamsham Prem Kumar, Konduru Jaswanth, Kola Vishnu and Abhishek Kumar*

School of Electronics and Electrical Engineering, Lovely Professional University, Punjab, India

Abstract

Agriculture plays an important role in India, due to its vast population and the quality of its irrigation soil. This project proposes the improvement that can be made in the Irrigation system in a smart way using present-era technology. A Smart Irrigation System using Machine Learning Techniques is a prototype-based project which gives the basic idea to make changes and improvement in our old traditional irrigation methods to reduce the use of water as well as the manpower in farming. The precise sensing of soil moisture sensor gives the input by providing enough amount of water to the field. It helps in improving the growth of plants and prevents overflow of water which reduces leaching and helps in areas where there is water scarcity. Moreover, the other parameter it has is a temperature sensor which provides us with the accurate temperature of soil. Further, the prototype has an Arduino UNO board which helps us to display the input and output readings on an LCD display and record the values in an Excel sheet to predict the decision using machine learning technique.

Keywords: Irrigation, water pump, smart agriculture, ANN, proteus, Arduino

9.1 Introduction

Water is required for optimum plant growth. An irrigation system is a method of artificially distributing water in agricultural fields [1]. To

Corresponding author: abkvjti@gmail.com

Abhishek Kumar, Suman Lata Tripathi, and K. Srinivasa Rao (eds.) Machine Learning for VLSI Chip Design, (139–160) © 2023 Scrivener Publishing LLC

maintain soil moisture, irrigation systems are used mostly in arid and low-rainfall areas. It aids in the reduction of weed growth in the field. There are two types of irrigation: traditional irrigation and modern irrigation. Check basin, furrow irrigation, basin irrigation, and strip irrigation are the most common irrigation methods. It makes use of watering cans, buckets, pumps, and canals, among other things. The technique requires a significant amount of labour for weeding, irrigation, and fertilisation, but it is not based on knowledge [2]. Modern irrigation has been developed to improve the irrigation system. Drip irrigation, sprinkler irrigation, and pot irrigation are the three types. Without the aid of technology, the existing modern irrigation system is unable to anticipate the real amount of water required for crops. It can result in either under irrigation—the soil moisture will be affected by irrigation, and the crop may be killed—or excess irrigation, which causes crop diseases and clogs. Both will have an impact on yield output. ML technologies aid in the efficient use of water, conservation, and improvement of the quality and quantity of water. Monitoring and accessing the irrigation system remotely is also possible based on pre-processed data and real-time meteorological measurement using ML technologies. As a result, the farmer might take precautionary measures during the irrigation time. Automatic Irrigation System using Machine learning technique is a prototype which gives us the measures of soil moisture sensor and Arduino UNO board in Agricultural field. The input is detected from the soil with soil moisture sensor and senses the nature of soil, i.e., either dry soil or wet soil, and instruct the Arduino UNO board [3] to action required for water and getting the output in the form of water flow to the soil. For instance, if the nature of the soil is dry, then the motor pump will automatically run till the soil turns moist or wet.

This work is focused on bringing down the wastage of water and manpower. It also improves the growth of plants because we are reducing leaching by providing sufficient amount of water to the plant. The availability of water for irrigation in some parts of rural areas is much less, so to give proper watering to the field we can implement this project which can be worked in real life. The design is versatile because the package may be modified at any time. It will thus be created to meet the particular needs of the user [4]. This makes the projected system cost-effective and moveable and an occasional maintenance resolution for small-scale agriculturists in rural areas. In this work the input of soil moisture sensor is mapped on a variable resistor. If the resistance value is more than 70%, then the motor pump will get on and it displays on the LCD display. And if the resistance value is less than 70% and more than 30%, we are giving this value as moist

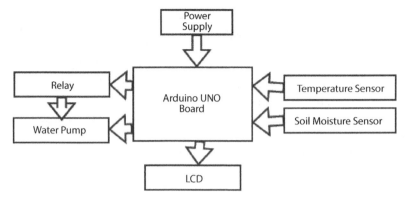

Figure 9.1 Block diagram.

level, just to say that the soil is not dry and has some water moisture in it and maybe it gets dry soon. Moving further, if the resistance value is less than 30%, then the indication on display will be as WET soil and pump is OFF. To indicate the temperature of soil, we used a Temperature sensor. The input is taken from the temperature sensor and the value is displayed on the LCD with the help of Arduino UNO board. Moreover, we have used a relay and a BC547 transistor to control the operation of the motor pump which is always connected to a battery. If the switch of the motor is not in ON condition, then the LED and sounder provided will give us indication that the motor button is OFF. The Arduino program which we have given works in the Proteus software only after providing the hex file of that particular Arduino program into the Arduino board in the Proteus software. On the other hand, soil moisture sensor also requires a HEX file to operate in virtual condition. A Machine learning algorithm has been implemented so that the data of the soil moisture sensor, Temperature sensor and pump motor is recorded in an Excel sheet for every 30-min time period. Figure 9.1 presents the block diagram of the work.

9.2 Hardware Module

9.2.1 Soil Moisture Sensor

Soil moisture, soil temperature, humidity, meteorological conditions, leaf sensing, and canopy temperature are all examples of sensor devices used to measure environmental conditions. The deployed environmental sensors in irrigation measure the real-time values. The soil wetness sensing element is one sensing element used to gauge the meter content of water inside the soil, because the straight gravimetric dimension of soil wetness desires eliminating, drying, still as sample weight [4]. Figure 9.2 shows the sensors detect the water content not in a direct way with the assistance of another rule of soil like dielectric constant, resistance, otherwise interaction with neutrons, and replacement of the wetness content.

The relation among the calculated property also as wetness of soil ought to be adjusted and could modify supported ecological factors like temperature, style of soil, otherwise electrical physical phenomenon. The microwave emission that is mirrored is influenced by the wetness of soil also as in the main employed in agriculture and remote sensing among geophysical science.

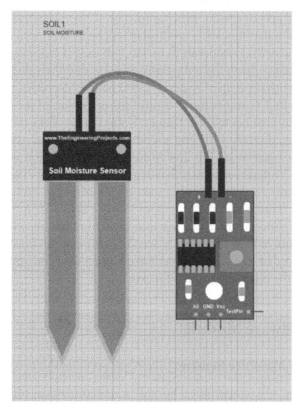

Figure 9.2 Soil moisture sensor [5].

9.2.2   LM35-Temperature Sensor

Temperature sensor in Figure 9.3 is LM35, which works on a range from -55°C to 150°C. The output of LM35 is digital in Proteus software and has various applications [12].

9.2.3   POT Resistor

A potentiometer is a manually adjustable resistance with three terminals shown in Figure 9.4(a) and 9.4(b). Two of the terminals are connected to the other ends of a resistive part, and therefore the third terminal connects to a slippy contact, known as a wiper, moving over the resistive part.

The potentiometer basically functions as a variable resistance divider. The resistive part is seen as two resistors asynchronous (the total potentiometer resistance), wherever the wiper position determines the resistance magnitude relation of the primary electrical device to the second electrical device. If a reference voltage is applied across the top terminals, the position of the wiper determines the output voltage of the potentiometer. A potentiometer is additionally referred to as a potmeter or pot.

9.2.4   BC-547 Transistor

BC-547 is a NPN semiconductor device; therefore the collector and emitter are going to be left open (Reverse biased) once the base pin is command

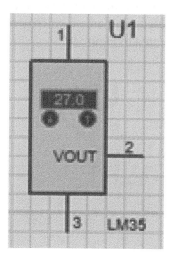

Figure 9.3 Temperature sensor [6].

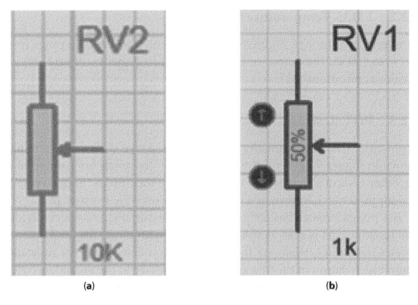

(a)   (b)

Figure 9.4 (a) POT resistor [7], (b) Variable POT resistor [7].

at ground and can be closed (Forward biased) once a signal is provided to base pin.

9.2.5 Sounder

Sounder is normally used for giving some indication and normally this indication is some kind of a warning. Proteus has a built-in component for a sounder; it is an animated component which gives a sound (beep) when it is turned ON, as presented in Figure 9.5.

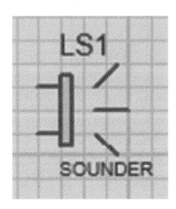

Figure 9.5 Sounder [8].

9.2.6 LCD 16x2

LCD stands for liquid show. Sixteen×2 digital display means that it has 16 Columns and a pair of Rows as shown in Figure 9.6. There are area unit tons of mixtures out there like 8×1, 8×2, 10×2, 16×1, etc.; however, the foremost used one is the 16×2 digital display. So, it will have 16×2 = thirty two characters in total and every character is fabricated from 5×8 constituent Dots [11].

9.2.7 Relay

A Relay is a simple electromechanical switch as presented in Figure 9.7. While we use normal switches to shut or open a circuit manually, a relay is additionally a switch that connects or disconnects two circuits. However, rather than a manual operation, a relay uses an associate electrical signal to

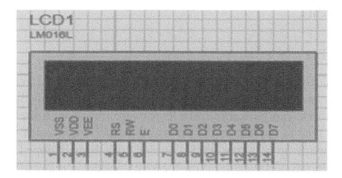

Figure 9.6 LCD display 16x2 [9].

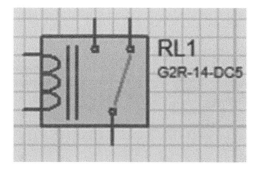

Figure 9.7 Relay [9].

regulate electro magnet, that successively connects or disconnects another circuit.

A relay works on an electromagnetic induction principle. When an electromagnet is applied with some current, it produces a magnetic field around it. DC current to the load is applied by A switch copper coil and the iron core acts as electromagnet. When coil is applied with DC current, it starts attracting contact. This is known as energizing of relay. When supply is removed it returns to the original position. This is known as de-energizing.

9.2.8   Push Button

Human Machine Interface (HMI) management panels principally use this kind of push buttons as shown in Figure 9.8(a) and 9.8(b); they are known as as membrane switches. All the data input device sort mobile phones conjointly use membrane sort push buttons. Digital clocks, watches, alarms, most of the electronic gadgets that offer Human Interface, use these switches.

9.2.9   LED

It is primarily just a specialised sort of diode as they need very similar electrical characteristics to a PN junction diode. This suggests that a light-emitting diode can pass current in its forward direction; however, it can block the flow of current in the reverse direction. Light-emitting diodes area unit made up of a very skinny layer of fairly heavily doped semiconductor material and reckoning on the semiconductor material used and also the quantity of doping, once forward biased an LED can emit a colored light at a selected spectral wavelength shown in Figure 9.9.

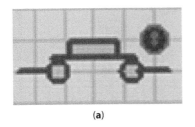 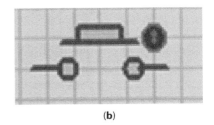

(a)   (b)

Figure 9.8 (a) Push button OFF, (b) Push button ON [9].

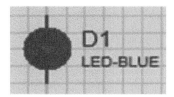

Figure 9.9 LED [9].

9.2.10   Motor

A DC motor is a simple motor that should have polarity distinction at both ends as presented in Figure 9.10. If this polarity is in forward direction, then the DC motor moves in one direction and if we have a tendency to reverse the polarity then the DC motor moves the other way.

Figure 9.11 presents the interfaced circuit with all components which is useful in real life scenarios in an agriculture field, organic farming, gardening, etc. In case of a very large agriculture field, we can put one or two soil moisture sensors in 1 acre of land, so that we do it in a cost-efficient way and achieve the results without manpower and can save a lot of water. The same procedure can be followed for organic farming as well. People who go to an office daily might not get enough time to water their plants in the garden but can get it done with a smart irrigation system, which can be monitored from anywhere in the world and keeps the switch of the motor ON as it goes ON only when the soil is dry.

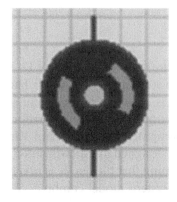

Figure 9.10 Motor [9].

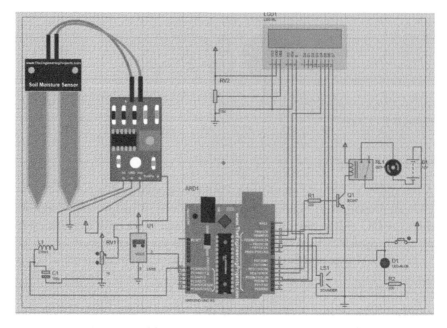

Figure 9.11 Project circuit.

9.3   Software Module

Rapid implementation means immediate, just weeks to a full solution compared to months or years when using data mining, cubes and hard-coding. There are low acquisition costs and low life-cycle colts – perpetual licenses, established maintenance and support and easy configuration for changes in underlying data or new requirements. It reduces and eliminates most training costs since data is organized.

9.3.1   Proteus Tool

Proteus software structure is shown in Figure 9.12. Proteus could be a complete embedded system software system, and a hardware style simulation platform, Proteus ISIS, is an associate intelligent schematic input system, system style and Simulation of the essential platform to attain the mixture of single-chip microcomputer simulation and PSpice circuit simulation. The schematic diagram designed in ISIS will automatically export the network table once confirming that the device is prepackaged properly.

The Proteus virtual system model combines SPICE circuit simulation of mixed mode, dynamic device and microcontroller model to understand

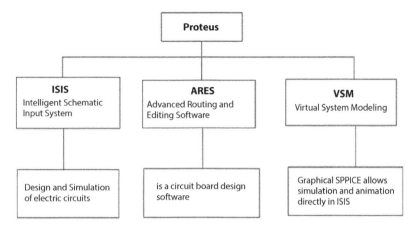

Figure 9.12 Proteus flow chart.

the whole cooperative simulation supported microcontroller style [10]. For the primary time, it is doable to develop and take a look at such styles before the physical model comes out. The Proteus package product embraces Proteus VSM, VSM for ARM7/LPC2XXX, VSM for 51/52, VSM for AVR, VSM for PIC24, Proteus PCB style, Advanced Simulation Feature (ASF). Proteus could be an immense teaching resource, which might be utilized in the teaching and experiment of analogue and digital circuits, microcontroller and embedded system software package, integrated experiment of microcontroller system, innovative experiment and graduation style, project style and merchandise development. Proteus is extremely appropriate for talent analysis and electronic competition. It is necessary and tough to gauge the abilities of a single-chip digital computer. Proteus will offer all the resources required for the check, directly assess the correctness of hardware circuit style, directly right the code with hardware schematic diagram, verify the perform of the entire style, and take a look at governable, simple to judge and straightforward to implement. There square measure wide sensible used cases from Proteus [11].

9.3.2 Arduino Based Prototyping

The Arduino prototyping board presented in Figure 9.13 is associated with open supply small controller which may be simply programmed, erased and reprogrammed at any instant of your time. Introduced in 2005, the Arduino platform was designed to produce a reasonable and simple approach for hobbyists, students and professionals to form devices that move with their

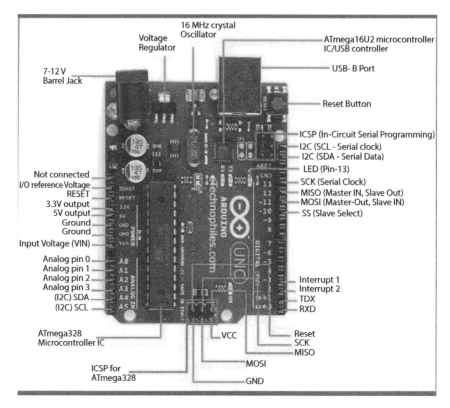

Figure 9.13 Arduino UNO.

setting mistreatment sensors and actuators. Supported easy small controller boards, it is associated with open supply computing platform that is used for constructing and programming electronic devices. It is additionally capable of acting as a mini PC rather like different small controllers by taking inputs and dominant the outputs for a range of physics devices [12]. It is conjointly capable of receiving and causing info over the web with the assistance of assorted Arduino shields. Arduino uses a hardware referred to as the Arduino development board and computer code for developing the code referred to as the Arduino IDE (Integrated Development Environment). designed with the 8-bit Atmel AVR microcontrollers that are factory-made by Atmel or a 32-bit Atmel ARM, these microcontrollers are programmed simply using the C or C++ language within the Arduino IDE [3].

Connect all the components placed on the schematic layout with wire by clicking on one terminal of the component with the next terminal of the other component. Compile the below Arduino program by clicking on the shown arrow symbol in Figure 9.14 [13].

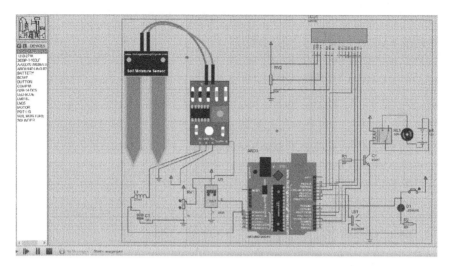

Figure 9.14 Components on layout.

```
void loop()
{
lcd.clear();
val = analogRead(T_Sensor); //Read Temperature
sensor value
int mv = ( val/1024.0)*5000;
cel = mv/10;
int Moisture = analogRead(M_Sensor); //Read
Moisture Sensor Value
lcd.setCursor(0,0);
lcd.print("TEMP:");
lcd.setCursor(5,0);
lcd.print(cel);
lcd.setCursor(7,0);
lcd.print("*C");
if (Moisture> 700)   // for dry soil
{
lcd.setCursor(11,0);
lcd.print("DRY");
lcd.setCursor(11,1);
lcd.print("SOIL");
if (digitalRead(W_led)==1) //test the availability of
water in storage
```

```
{
digitalWrite(13, HIGH);
lcd.setCursor(0,1);
lcd.print("PUMP:ON");
}
else
{
digitalWrite(13, LOW);
lcd.setCursor(0,1);
lcd.print("PUMP:OFF");
tone(Speaker, NOTE_C4, 500);
delay(500);
tone(Speaker, NOTE_D4, 500);
delay(500);
tone(Speaker, NOTE_E4, 500);
delay(500);
tone(Speaker, NOTE_F4, 500);
delay(500);
tone(Speaker, NOTE_G4, 500);
delay(500);
}
}
if (Moisture>= 300 && Moisture<=700) //for
Moist Soil
{
lcd.setCursor(11,0);
lcd.print("MOIST");
lcd.setCursor(11,1);
lcd.print("SOIL");
digitalWrite(13,LOW);
lcd.setCursor(0,1);
lcd.print("PUMP:OFF");
}
if (Moisture < 300) // For Wet soil
{
lcd.setCursor(11,0);
lcd.print("WET");
lcd.setCursor(11,1);
lcd.print("SOIL");
digitalWrite(13,LOW);
```

```
lcd.setCursor(0,1);
lcd.print("PUMP:OFF");
}
delay(100);
}
```

Copy the HEX file location from the console window below the program which is shown in the red coloured box. Paste the HEX file location in the Arduino UNO R3 board in the Proteus software, which is shown in the red coloured box in Figure 9.15. We need to add one more HEX file to the soil moisture sensor which will be available while downloading the library file of soil moisture sensor. So, we need to add that HEX file in the following blue box shown in Figure 9.16. After completing all the above steps we can proceed to run the implementation. After the successful implementation of the Proteus software and Arduino program the following results will be obtained by running the Proteus schematic.

1) After clicking on the Run button below, the program will start running by switching ON the LCD and displaying: "Project By Anil, Jaswanth, Prem, Vishnu" shown in Figure 9.15.
2) If the soil moisture value is below 70% and above 30% in the variable POT resistor which will be the value of soil moisture sensor. In this case, we are taking the soil moisture value as

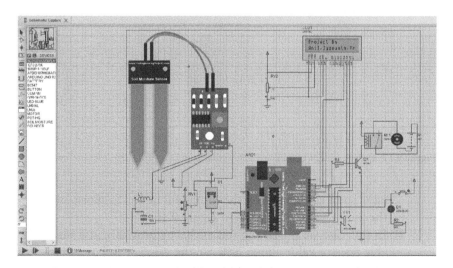

Figure 9.15 Powered interfaced module.

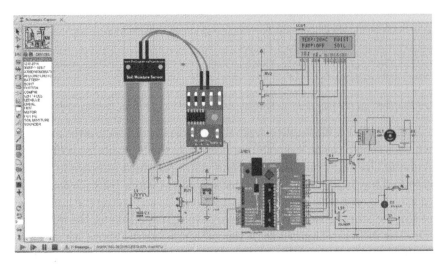

Figure 9.16 Output on moist condition.

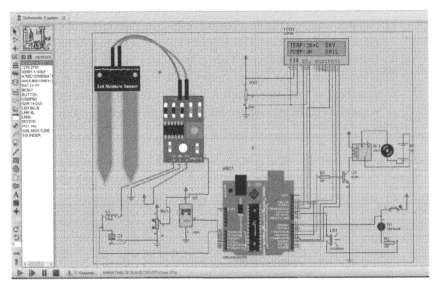

Figure 9.17 Output on dry condition.

58%, so in this condition the result will be soil as moist and the pump is OFF as shown in Figure 9.16.

3) In this case we are taking soil as dry by providing the variable resistor value above 70%. So, the value of soil moisture sensor is 75% and temperature value is 20°C. Now, the result

will be shown as soil is dry, temperature is 20°C and pump is as shown in Figure 9.17.

4) In the final case we are taking the variable resistor value to below 30% and see the results. Here, the soil moisture sensor value is 25% and the temperature value as 25°C. The result will be displaying as the Pump is off due to wet soil and temperature as 25°C.

9.4   Machine Learning (Ml) Into Irrigation

Machine learning, by its definition, is a field of technology that evolved from finding out pattern recognition and procedure learning theory in AI. It is the training and building of algorithms that may learn from and create predictions on knowledge sets. These procedures operate by construction of a model from example inputs so as to create data-driven predictions or selections, Instead of following firm static program directions, the method starts with feeding smart quality knowledge then coaching our machines (computers) by building machine learning models that can exploit the info and totally different algorithms [13–15]. Machine learning involves two tasks: (a) supervised machine learning: The program is "trained" on a predefined set of "training examples", that then facilitate its ability to succeed in Associate in Nursing correct conclusion once given new knowledge, and (b) Unsupervised machine learning: The program is given a bunch of knowledge and should notice patterns and relationships.

Machine learning and neural network techniques are commonly used in irrigation systems. It comes in a variety of forms and employs a variety of principles. In the input layer, multiple parameters are presented as inputs. For a better result, the input layer has more than one node or neuron. It could be the stages of a plant's development or several forms of environmental factors. The concealed layer is then added after the input layer. It gets data from each node in the input layer. After that, the output layer is placed on top of the hidden layer as shown in Figure 9.18, which displays the desired or predicted outcome based on the hidden layer's training data. In the input layer we can see that there are two inputs; first input can be considered as soil moisture sensor, and the second input is temperature sensor which are shown in green colour [16, 17]. On further step, the inputs are taken into different kinds of hidden layers, where the actual algorithm of machine learning is done like the acquiring of input data, processing them into software, and so on. This hidden layer cannot be seen

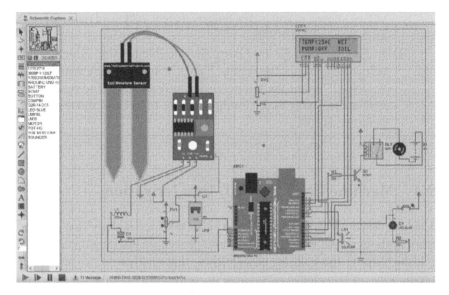

Figure 9.18 Output in wet condition.

at the front end, so all the data from the hidden layer is combined together and processed to get the output in an spreadsheet file [8]. This works on project made in hardware mode, so that we can get accurate results. Here, we have taken the sample data from the research websites and stored them in an Excel file because of software implementation [9].

Generated dataset from a sensor can process for the prediction of results in different cases. Artificial neural network requires a dataset for the training [18, 19]; it identifies the hidden characteristic of the data and trains the model accordingly. The model shown in Figure 9.19 is implemented

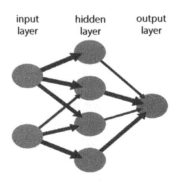

Figure 9.19 Neural network algorithm [18].

in Python. The trained data faces the challenge of testing set products the decision and updating the farmers in advance to avoid losses. Dataset of SMEX03 Soil Moisture, Meteorological, and Vegetation Data: Brazil has been used to train the ANN model. It contained the average moisture indicator temperature at 11 different places in the field and reads the seven different readings per day. The minimum moisture level of the soil and higher temperature value the indictor to have water and staus is predicted and '1'-motor pump ON or else OFF. Figures 9.20(a) and 9.20(b) plot the model train and loss vs. epochs; for the epoch value of 100 the loss falls to 0.4. The model can make correct decisions 55% of the time.

```
[[ 0  9]
 [ 0 11]]
TP= 11
FP= 9
TN= 0
FN= 0
accuracy
0.55
classification_error
0.44999999999999996
sensitivity
1.0
specificity
0.0
false_positive_rate
1.0
precision
0.55
ROC AUC: 0.500000
dict_keys(['loss', 'accuracy', 'val_loss', 'val_accuracy'])
```

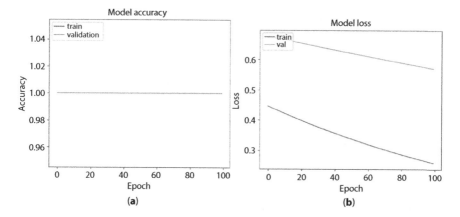

Figure 9.20 (a) Accuracy vs. epoch, (b) Loss vs. epoch.

9.5   Conclusion

In Irrigation, Soil moisture is a very important parameter in developing smart irrigation. Although moisture sensor gets corrosion within a few years, the precise value it gives to provide the water shows the importance of using it in large fields. When machine learning is used in agriculture, the irrigation system is improved. It assists in the effective use of water and the reduction of water waste. This knowledge-based system combines automated data analysis, data recording, and decision-making with machine learning implementation. It boosts crop output and quality. This project proposes a Smart Irrigation system using machine learning technique along with the Arduino program in which the input values like soil moisture, temperature are taken, then compared with the logic in the program, and the Arduino board gives the motor pump to turn ON or OFF with respect to level of moisture in the soil. Later, with machine learning algorithm these results are stored in an Excel sheet where the data is updated every 30 minutes. The project is very effective and easy to use by farmers once someone teaches them how it works, and any changes can be made according the required parameters.

References

1. Chen, Y., Gu, H., & Liang, Y. (2012). Application of Proteus virtual simulation in the teaching of Microcomputer Principle. *Technology and application of computer, 38*(1), 106-108.
2. Jain, A., Goel, M., Jain, S., Kumar, S., Agarwal, A., & Jadoun, V. K. (2022). Microcontroller based ATM monitoring system for security purpose. *Materials Today: Proceedings, 51,* 894-899.
3. Arduino, L. (2015). Arduino introduction. Arduino [Online]. Available: http://arduino. cc/en/guide/introduction.
4. https://components101.com/microcontrollers/arduino-uno
5. Alpaydın E (2010). *Introduction to machine learning.* MIT Press, Cambridge, MA.
6. Eller, H., & Denoth, A. (1996). A capacitive soil moisture sensor. *Journal of Hydrology, 185*(1-4), 137-146.
7. Singla, B., Mishra, S., Singh, A., & Yadav, S. (2019). A study on smart irrigation system using IoT. *International Journal of Advance Research, Ideas and Innovations in Technology, 5*(2), 1416-1418.
8. Kumar, M. S., Chandra, T. R., Kumar, D. P., & Manikandan, M. S. (2016, January). Monitoring moisture of soil using low cost homemade Soil moisture sensor and Arduino UNO. In *2016 3rd international conference on*

advanced computing and communication systems (ICACCS) (Vol. 1, pp. 1-4). IEEE.

9. Drusch, M., Moreno, J., Del Bello, U., Franco, R., Goulas, Y., Huth, A., ... & Verhoef, W. (2016). The fluorescence explorer mission concept—ESA's earth explorer 8. *IEEE Transactions on Geoscience and Remote Sensing, 55*(3), 1273-1284.

10. Tyagi, A., Gupta, N., Navani, J. P., Tiwari, M. R., & Gupta, M. A. (2017). Smart irrigation system. *International Journal for Innovative Research in Science & Technology, 3*(10).

11. Shwetha, N., Niranjan, L., Gangadhar, N., Jahagirdar, S., Suhas, A. R., & Sangeetha, N. (2021, October). Efficient Usage of water for smart irrigation system using Arduino and Proteus design tool. In *2021 2nd International Conference on Smart Electronics and Communication (ICOSEC)* (pp. 54-61). IEEE.

12. Nandhini, R., Poovizhi, S., Jose, P., Ranjitha, R., & Anila, S. (2017, March). Arduino based smart irrigation system using IoT. In *3rd National Conference on Intelligent Information and Computing Technologies (IICT '17)* (pp. 1-5).

13. Oduntan, O. E., & Hammed, M. (2018). A Predictive Model for Improving Cereals Crop Productivity Using Supervised Machine Learning Algorithm. 1-11.

14. Khoshnevisan, B., Rafiee, S., Omid, M., Mousazadeh, H., & Rajaeifar, M. A. (2014). Application of artificial neural networks for prediction of output energy and GHG emissions in potato production in Iran. *Agricultural Systems, 123*, 120-127.

15. C.M. Bishop, *Neural Networks for Pattern Recognition*, Oxford University Press, Oxford, 1995.

16. B.D. Ripley, *Pattern Recognition and Neural Networks*, Cambridge University Press, Cambridge, 1996.

17. Su S. L., Singh D. N., Baghini M. S., A critical review of soil moisture measurement, 2014; 54: 92–105.

18. Kanade, P., & JP, P. (2021). Arduino based Machine Learning and IoT Smart Irrigation System. *International Journal of Soft Computing and Engineering (IJSCE), 10*(4), 1-5.

19. Lata Tripathi, S., & Dwivedi, S. (Eds.). (2022). *Electronic Devices and Circuit Design: Challenges and Applications in the Internet of Things* (1st ed.). Apple Academic Press. https://doi.org/10.1201/9781003145776. ISBN: 9781771889933

10

Design of Smart Wheelchair with Health Monitoring System

Narendra Babu Alur¹*, Kurapati Poorna Durga¹, Boddu Ganesh¹, Manda Devakaruna¹, Lakkimsetti Nandini¹, A. Praneetha², T. Satyanarayana¹ and K. Girija Sravani³†

¹Department of Electronics and Communication Engineering, and Engineering, Lakireddy Bali Reddy College of Engineering (Autonomous), Mylavaram, Krishna District, AP, India
²Department of Computer Science Engineering, Lakireddy Bali Reddy College of Engineering (Autonomous), Mylavaram, Krishna District, AP, India
³Department of Electronics and Communication Engineering, KLEF, Vaddeswaram, Green Fields, Andhra Pradesh, India

Abstract

The human body is precious. Each and every part of our body plays a great role in our life. The absence of any one of them makes our life complex. The life of a handicapped person is vulnerable. Especially the persons with locomotive defects, who depend on others to move from one place to another. To solve this problem, the wheelchair was invented. To push the wheelchair, another person is required. In order to avoid this, the concept of a smart wheelchair is introduced. Using this smart wheelchair, the disabled person can move from one place to other independently. This wheelchair works based on the movements of the person's head. The person can move the chair on his own just by moving his head in the required direction. An accelerometer sensor senses the head movements of the person and based on that data the chair is moved accordingly. Additionally, this model offers continuous health monitoring of the patient. This monitoring includes collecting the heartbeat rate and temperature of the person continuously, and any change from regular readings will be communicated to the doctor for remote treatment of the patient. This project helps the disabled person as well as his relatives by

*Corresponding author: narendrababualu@gmail.com
†Corresponding author: kondavitee.sravani03@gmail.com

Abhishek Kumar, Suman Lata Tripathi, and K. Srinivasa Rao (eds.) Machine Learning for VLSI Chip Design, (161–170) © 2023 Scrivener Publishing LLC

reducing human intervention to push the wheelchair and is also helpful in monitoring the health of the person.

Keywords: Disability, wheelchair, accelerometer sensor, head movements, health monitoring

10.1   Introduction

The number of physically challenged people is increasing day by day. This trend may be due to increased accidents or increased ageing effect in people or by virtue of birth. Due to these disabilities people are becoming dependent on others, especially the people with locomotive defects. It is not possible for an individual to depend on others for their basic needs all the time. Also, the health of these people must be continuously monitored, including regular visits to the doctor. But under such circumstances, it is difficult for them to do this. Therefore, an autonomous machine must be invented to solve this problem.

The human body is precious. Each and every part of our body plays a great role in our life. The absence of any one of them makes our life complex. The life of a handicapped person is vulnerable. Especially the persons with locomotive defects, who depend on others to move from one place to another. To solve this problem, the wheelchair was invented. To push the wheelchair another person is required. In order to avoid this, the concept of a smart wheelchair is introduced. Using this smart wheelchair, the disabled person can move from one place to another independently. This wheelchair works based on the movements of the person's head. The person can move the chair on his own just by moving his head in the required direction. An accelerometer sensor senses the head movements of the person and based on that data the chair is moved accordingly. Additionally, this model offers continuous health monitoring of the patient. This health monitoring includes collecting the heartbeat rate and temperature of the person continuously, and any change from regular readings will be communicated to the doctor for remote treatment of the patient. This project helps the disabled person as well as his relatives by reducing human intervention to push the wheelchair and is also helpful in monitoring the health of the person.

In this proposed model, the accelerometer sensor is connected to the LPC2148 to detect the head movement of the person sitting in the chair and move it accordingly. The PPG sensor and temperature sensor are used to continuously record the oxygen levels and temperature of a person.

If any outliers are found, the system communicates with the doctor for remote treatment. The emergency alert system is also attached to the wheelchair, so any discrepancies can be communicated to loved ones by phone or message.

10.2   Proposed Methodology

A considerable amount of research has already been done on the wheelchair in terms of controlling a machine without human intervention. Initially, the wheelchair is moved autonomously using a joystick [8] where the user is given a remote-like device, and then he or she can operate it themselves. The joystick is provided with directional buttons and a speed control system for controlling the motion of the wheelchair. The same process is implemented by replacing the joystick with a smartphone [1]. Sensor characteristics and utilisation can be understood from Narendra Metal [9]. Using the tilt sensor in the smartphone, one can move the chair autonomously. This system also includes controlling the chair using voice and human gestures. All these features are controlled using a smartphone. This system also includes smoke, gas, and temperature sensors to detect any unwanted situation around or in the user. Apart from these we can add other features like controlling the height of the footrest, detecting the outside weather to decide whether to go out or not, automatic opening head mats or umbrella in case of rain. These features are discussed in [8].

This system can also be realised with a voice recognition system. The commands are given by the user and the wheelchair moves accordingly [4] discusses the same thing as it includes giving the commands in a regional language. In real time this process may not work out well with handicapped or paralysed people who are unable to speak clearly.

Face recognition is used for moving the wheelchair [6]. With the help of a camera the images of the user are continuously clicked and compared with predefined images, and based on those results the wheelchair is moved. This is limited to a single user, i.e., the wheelchair can be used only by one particular user. This process may not work efficiently during nighttime due to lack of lighting.

Beyond all these we can make use of human gestures which are identical to every user. An autonomous moving wheelchair operated by hand movements is discussed in [7]. This involves moving the wheelchair based on hand movements. An accumulator unit will be recording the hand movements and sends this data to a motor driver unit for moving the wheelchair. In this case, a completely paralysed person or a person without hands cannot make use of this system or even a system that includes a joystick. Keeping all this in mind, head movements are considered for moving the wheelchair [2]. The head movements of the user are detected using an accelerometer sensor and are sent to the motor driver unit for motion of the chair.

Also, an obstacle detection system must be introduced in order to stop the wheelchair from being damaged. This problem can be avoided by using ultrasonic sensors as they detect an object at a particular distance and stop the wheelchair [8].

Systems that can monitor the user's health condition on a continuous basis are more beneficial. Health monitoring and sharing the details with a doctor is explained in [10, 11]. [3, 5, 12, 13] Using sensors the temperature and heartbeat of the user are continuously recorded and sent to the doctor; if any abnormalities are found, remote or immediate treatment is advised [1]. A panic button is added to inform loved ones that the user has a problem. In case of an emergency, the user can press the panic button so that a message is sent to the predefined number informing the recipient that the user is in difficulties and requires immediate attention.

In this proposed system, wheelchair motion using head gestures is implemented by interfacing them with LPC2148. This also includes a health monitoring system as in [5] and an obstacle detection system using ultrasonic sensors. An emergency alert system through a message to the predefined number is also used. This idea is implemented using LPC2148 board instead of Arduino. Arduino is slower when compared to LPC2148 and also requires more power supply than LPC2148.

10.3   The Proposed System

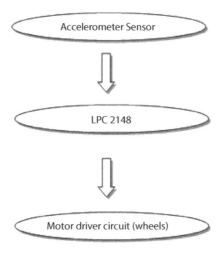

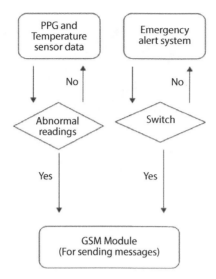

The proposed hardware components for the System setup.

An LPC board as shown in Figure 10.1 is used to provide interfacing between accelerometer and motor driver circuit for motion of the wheelchair. Also, the data regarding health monitoring is processed using LPC board only.

The accelerometer sensor as shown in Figure 10.2 is used to detect the tilt angle of the head. Here five types of states can be defined, namely right, left, front, back, stop.

The processed accelerometer data is sent to the motor driver circuit, hence moving the wheelchair. The motor driver circuit is shown in Figure 10.3. A single motor driver circuit can drive two wheels.

An ultrasonic sensor as shown in Figure 10.4 is used in an obstacle detection system. Whenever an obstacle is found in the way, the ultrasonic

Figure 10.1 Schematic view of the board.

Figure 10.2 Schematic view of accelerometer sensor.

Figure 10.3 Schematic view of motor driver circuit.

Figure 10.4 Schematic view of ultrasonic sensor.

sensor senses it and immediately stops the wheelchair to avoid collision with the obstacle.

The pulse oximeter sensor shown in Figure 10.5 consists of a heartbeat and oxygen level detecting sensor. It also measures the temperature of the human body when put in contact with a body. When nothing is in contact with it, it detects the surrounding temperature.

The GSM module shown in Figure 10.6 is used to send messages to a predefined number. When temperature or oxygen level or heartbeat of the user crosses the threshold value then a message is sent to the doctor with the relevant health parameters. Also, when the user clicks the panic button a message is sent to his relatives informing tthem that the user has a problem.

Figure 10.5 Schematic view of pulse oximeter sensor.

Figure 10.6 Schematic view of GSM module.

Software:

1. Keil micro vision software
2. Flash magic tool

10.4   Results and Discussions

Each module has been tested separately in the laboratory for proper functioning. Then, after connecting all the modules in a predefined procedure,
the prototype wheelchair is fabricated and the required results are achieved,
as shown in the Figures 10.7 and 10.8. The accelerometer sensor is inserted
in a cap and placed on the user's head. The pulse oximeter sensor is placed
on the handle of the wheelchair to maintain contact with the person's body.

Figure 10.7 The measurement setup.

Figure 10.8 The measurement setup.

A panic button is available for any abnormality in the patient's health condition or if he is in any distress, and correspondingly a message will be sent to a predefined number.

10.5   Conclusions

The proposed system is being tested and shows accurate results. The components used are of comparatively low cost, which makes the system cost effective. The proposed system also consumes less power and is faster than other systems. Commercial production of the proposed wheelchair could be a great replacement for imported ones and will help the disabled patients in our country.

This system can also be implemented using eye movements and brain controls for the motion of the wheelchair. We can also make a standing wheelchair that assists the user to stand without the support of others.

References

1. Khadilkar, S. U., & Wagdarikar, N. (2015, January). Android phone controlled voice, gesture and touch screen operated smart wheelchair. In *2015 International Conference on Pervasive Computing (ICPC)* (pp. 1-4). IEEE.
2. Nasif, S., & Khan, M. A. G. (2017, December). Wireless head gesture controlled wheel chair for disable persons. In *2017 IEEE Region 10 Humanitarian Technology Conference (R10-HTC)* (pp. 156-161). IEEE.
3. Muthulakshmi, K., Indhu, M. R., & Lavanya, M. D. Healthcare Monitoring for Physically Challenged People in Wheelchair using IOT.
4. Chandramma R., Akshatha K. Gowda, Asha U., Jyothi B. S., and Meghana B. Bapat. Speech controlled smart wheel chair using regional languages.
5. D. Souza, D. J., Srivastava, S., Prithika, R., & SahanaRai, A. N. (2019). IoT based smart sensing wheelchair to assist in healthcare. *Methods*, 6(06).
6. Dongardive, Arun M. Smart Mobility System for Physically Handicap Using Labview, 2019.
7. Al-Wesabi, F. N., Alamgeer, M., Al-Yarimi, F., & Albaadani, A. (2019). A Smart-hand Movement-based System to Control a Wheelchair Wirelessly. *Sensors and Materials*, 31(9), 2947-2964.
8. Deepak Kumara, Reetu Malhotrab, and S. R. Sharma, Design and Construction of a Smart Wheelchair, 2020.
9. Narendra Babu, A, Thanuja Gonepudi, Rupakumari Macharla, Sirisha Vemula, and Suresh babu Tungala, Intelligent detection of vehicles during

poor vision, *Journal of Adv Research in Dynamical & Control Systems*, Vol. 12, Issue 02, 2020.

10. A. Narendrababu, S. Vyshnavi, D. Akhilandeswari, K. Pavan Kalyan, K. Akshay Kiran, E.V. Krishna Rao, and Y.S.V. Raman, Web Server Based Patient Monitoring System Using Lab VIEW, *Journal of Adv Research in Dynamical & Control Systems*, Vol. 12, Issue 02, 2020.

11. Badiganti P.K., Peddirsi S., Rupesh A.T.J., Tripathi S.L. (2022) Design and Implementation of Smart Healthcare Monitoring System Using FPGA. In: Rawat S., Kumar A., Kumar P., Anguera J. (eds.) *Proceedings of First International Conference on Computational Electronics for Wireless Communications. Lecture Notes in Networks and Systems*, vol 329. Springer, Singapore. https://doi.org/10.1007/978-981-16-6246-1_18

12. Kanak Kumar, Soumyadeepa Bhaumik, and Suman Lata Tripathi, "Health Monitoring System", in *Electronic Device and Circuits Design Challenges to Implement Biomedical Applications*, Elsevier *2021*. Doi: https://doi.org/10.1016/B978-0-323-85172-5.00021-6

13. Kanak Kumar, Anchal Sharma, Suman Lata Tripathi, "Sensors and Their Application", in *Electronic Device and Circuits Design Challenges to Implement Biomedical Applications*, Elsevier 2021. https://doi.org/10.1016/B978-0-323-85172-5.00021-6

11

Design and Analysis of Anti-Poaching Alert System for Red Sandalwood Safety

K. Rani Rudrama[1]*, Mounika Ramala[1], Poorna sasank Galaparti[1], Manikanta Chary Darla[1], Siva Sai Prasad Loya[1] and K. Srinivasa Rao[2]

[1]*Department of Electronics and Communication Engineering, Lakireddy Bali Reddy College of Engineering (Autonomous), Mylavaram, Krishna District, AP, India*
[2]*Department of Electronics and Communication Engineering, KLEF, Vaddeswaram, Green Fields, Andhra Pradesh, India*

Abstract

In this modern world smuggling goods has become a common thing especially of important trees in forests, such as red sandalwood. This represents a huge threat to forest resources, inflicts enormous economic harm, and has a disastrous impact on the ecosystem around the world. This work offers a WSN-based microcontroller-based anti-poaching system capable of detecting theft and protecting forests from natural disasters by monitoring vibrations, location, smoke, and temperature produced by various sensors attached to trees/branches. A three-axis MEMS accelerometer is used as a tilt sensor to monitor the position of the tree, a sound sensor to detect the vibrations from the tree, and also a temperature to detect the wildfires and alert the user immediately and tell the exact location with the help of GPS module. A microcontroller is used along with PC so that the information can be uploaded. The main application of temperature and smoke sensors is not only alerting the system but also pumping the water with the help of water motor in the forest to tackle the fire immediately, which reduces the damage effectively.

Keywords: WSN technology, accelerometer, LM35 sensor, GPS technology, IoT

**Corresponding author*: ranirudrama12@gmail.com

Abhishek Kumar, Suman Lata Tripathi, and K. Srinivasa Rao (eds.) Machine Learning for VLSI Chip Design, (171–184) © 2023 Scrivener Publishing LLC

11.1 Introduction

The need to address illegal activities such as poaching and destroying of environmentally and economically valuable tree varieties like Rosewood, Teakwood, Pine trees, and Sandalwood in wooded areas has risen radically in recent years [4]. To address these issues, a number of initiatives have been undertaken by various stakeholders, including the Indian government. These include anti-poaching watches and/or private/government security personnel being recruited, trained, and deployed across forests [1]. The threat was to be eradicated by harsh sanctions for convicted criminals and additional inducements for anti-poaching initiatives which were started from 2012 to 2017. The goal of this project is to create a mobile WSN technology that will be used in a wireless sensor network. This system will be located on the parts of trees and will be capable of detecting theft as well as sending warning signals to a remote terminal via wireless media using IoT.

In this modern world, smuggling goods has become a common thing especially of important trees in forests, such as red sandalwood. This represents a huge threat to forest resources, inflicts enormous economic harm, and has a disastrous impact on the ecosystem around the world. This work offers a WSN-based microcontroller-based anti-poaching system capable of detecting theft and protecting forests from natural disasters by monitoring vibrations, location, smoke, and temperature produced by various sensors attached to trees/branches. A three-axis MEMS accelerometer is used as a tilt sensor to monitor the position of the tree, a sound sensor to detect the vibrations from the tree, and also a temperature to detect the wildfires and alert the user immediately and tell the exact location with the help of a GPS module. A microcontroller is used along with a PC so that the information can be uploaded. The main application of temperature and smoke sensors is not only alerting the system but also pumping the water with the help of water motor in the forest to tackle the fire immediately, which reduces the damage effectively.

All of the things that are connected to the internet in the Internet of Things can be divided into three categories [2]:

A. Things that collect and then transmit data.
B. Things that receive and act on information.
C. Things that perform both functions.

A. Things that collect and then transmit data.

Temperature sensors, moisture sensors, motion sensors, smoke sensors, illuminance sensors, and so on are some examples of sensors. These sensors, when combined with a link, enable us to automatically collect data from the environment, allowing us to make more informed decisions.

B. Things that receive and act on information.

We are all familiar with machines that gather data and then function. Your car keys send a signal to your car, which causes the doors to unlock. When a paper is sent to your printer, it is printed. The list goes on and on. Furthermore, we can view the status of devices from anywhere in the world with an internet connection.

C. Things that perform both functions.

This group includes devices that transmit collected data and take actions based on that data. When devices can do both things, the Internet of Things becomes truly powerful. Things that gather and transmit data, as well as those that receive data and act on it.

11.2   Various Existing Proposed Anti-Poaching Systems

In this section, we have highlighted some available methods for setting up an anti-poaching system using WSN technology and connecting different devices to the internet of things, which will highlight our method that we implemented in this work.

Object detection has become a simple task as a result of recent technical breakthroughs in the advanced technologies such as Internet of Things (IoT) and Deep Learning. Poaching, which is a constant threat to forest creatures, has rendered them defenceless [1–4]. The purpose of our study is to come up with a practical approach to anti-poaching. Poachers have become money-making enterprises in the illegal market due to the rising need for boasting of pride in owning animal assets. The outcome of our solution provides the most appropriate way to minimise animal poaching through the use of Unmanned Aerial Vehicles (UAVs). Constant monitoring by park rangers would be a time-consuming activity that might not even be done correctly at times.

The goal of this chapter is to prohibit illicit forest assets exports that guard the environment [2]. Since the 1970s, forest assets (sandalwood and rosewood trees) has been victimised in the form of exporting. Sensors such as PIR and FIR are responsible to find the signal where any illegal poaching occurs, and this detected signal information is transmitted via wireless network communication to the concerned forest authorities, allowing them to order necessary action [5–10].

11.3 System Framework and Construction

The design of our proposed system is as shown in Figure 11.1, and the devices used in this model are described in this section. This framework makes use of the architecture described below.

Let's look at a quick rundown of all the components that go into making this device work.

A tilt sensor, as shown in Figure 11.2, is an instrument that measures the angle of an item in relation to a reference plane. Tilt sensors are used in a variety of applications to measure the tilting position in relation to gravity. They make it simple to identify inclination or orientation.

Gravity, vibration, temperature, acceleration/deceleration, shock, unobstructed line of sight between the user and the measured position, and tilt sensor calibration are all elements that affect tilt sensor functionality.

Arduino can be connected to PC by using USB and it communicates via serial port. Arduino uses its programming language similar to C++.

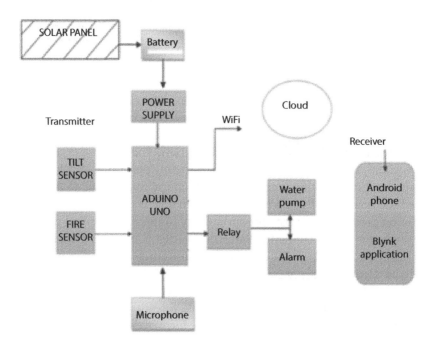

Figure 11.1 Block diagram of System Architecture.

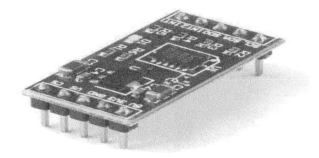

Figure 11.2 Schematic view of tilt sensor.

We can also use higher-level languages like Python and Java to control the devices. By using Python we can operate lights, sensors and switches and other devices in an effective way. There are 14 digital input/output pins, six analogue inputs, a 16 MHz quartz crystal, a USB connection, a power jack, an ICSP header, and a reset button on the board.

It is an actuator that senses sound waves through its intensity of receiving waves and converting it to electrical signals.

The sound sensor (Figure 11.3) is a component that includes a microphone and a processing circuit. This actuator is used to determine how loud a sound is. When a sound or noise is detected, the sensor generates an output signal in terms of voltage, which is transferred to a microcontroller, which subsequently does the required processing steps.

Figure 11.3 Schematic view of sound sensor.

Figure 11.4 Schematic view of GPS module.

The Global Positioning System (GPS) is a satellite-based system that measures and computes its position on Earth using satellites and ground stations [5]. For tracking or detecting a location, GPS receivers are commonly utilised in cell phones, fleet managing systems, and military applications. For accuracy, a GPS receiver must receive data from at least four satellites. The GPS receiver does not send any data to the satellites, and Figure 11.4 depicts the module.

This temperature sensor senses the temperature of the surroundings and measures in degree Celsius. The range of this sensor is -55°C to +150°C. There will be a change in accuracy of ±1/4°C.

It is a device used to display the results and outputs of various devices used in the system. 2*16 LCD means, 2 rows with 16 characters in each row [6]. +5V is the operating voltage of this LCD. It has 10 I/O pins contains of 8 data pins, register select and read/write pins.

A relay is a mechanical system which acts as a switch that is activated by an electrical current. The application of using relay is to transfer the current in one circuit which causes another circuit to open or close. Relays are employed when a circuit must be controlled by a separate signal or multiple circuits.

11.4 Results and Discussions

ThingView is an internet platform where we can store and retrieve data from the things or systems we are connected to. It is an open IoT platform and has MATLAB analytics.

In this ThingView platform, we can either access it in PC/laptop or mobile app for the purpose of storing and retrieving the data from the system. This platform will be connected to the cloud so that the real-time data can be updated accurately. Let us see how the app is used in this.

In the below Figure 11.5, we can observe the real-time readings of the system such as tilt sensor readings of X and Y axes, GPS co-ordinates latitude (LT) and longitude (LG), temperature reading and status of relay.

In order to show these outputs, we have written code with the help of Arduino IDE and backend code was given. So, with the instructions given in the program, the results are displayed in the application.

Working of the proposed method is shown in Figure 11.6 below.

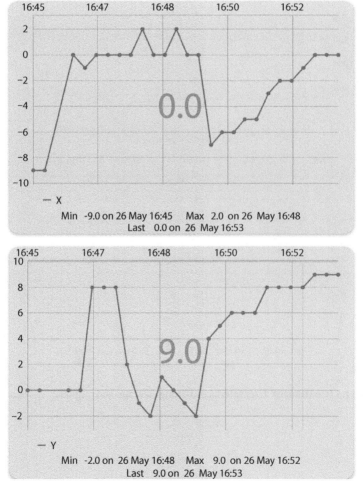

Figure 11.5 User interface of ThingView app and outputs.   (*Continued*)

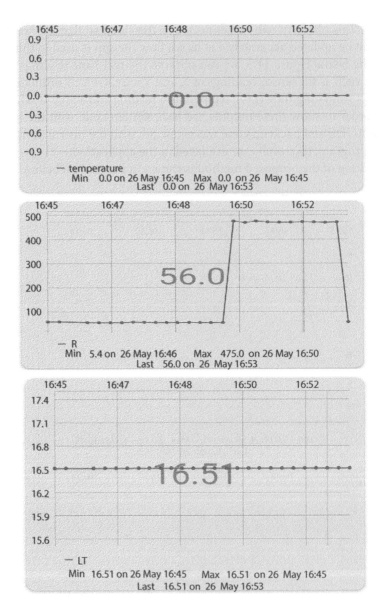

Figure 11.5 (Continued) User interface of ThingView app and outputs.   (*Continued*)

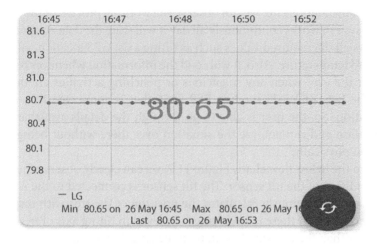

Figure 11.5 (Continued) User interface of ThingView app and outputs.

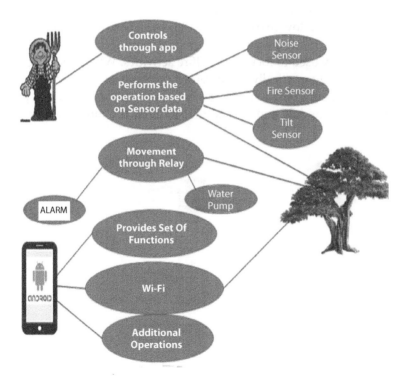

Figure 11.6 Implementation and working of system.

From the Figure 11.6, we can observe the working process of the system. As the system works continuously all day it will store the data continuously. It shows all the required values such as tilting axis, GPS location, vibration data and temperature. Also, it will send the information whenever required to alert the user when any suspicious or poaching activities are detected with the help of Wi-Fi module ESP 8266 that is connected to a mobile application. So, the user is able to go through the details available in the application and can analyze the situation over there without being at the location physically.

From the below flow chart, Figure 11.7, we can clearly observe the working condition of the tilt sensor. The tilt sensor is connected to the Arduino board and continuously calculates the position of the tree with respect to reference plane. If there is any change observed in tilting axis of tree which is greater than the threshold limit, then the Arduino will immediately send the updated values along with GPS location to the user android application and alert the user that the tree has fallen. So, the user can immediately take necessary actions to prevent the theft.

From the below flow chart, Figure 11.8, we can observe the working and implementation of temperature sensor in this project. The temperature sensor is mainly used to focus on wildfire activities. Whenever fire occurs near the tree, automatically temperature increases at the surroundings. Now, after noticing the increased levels immediately Arduino will give a signal to relay module and update the status in the mobile application.

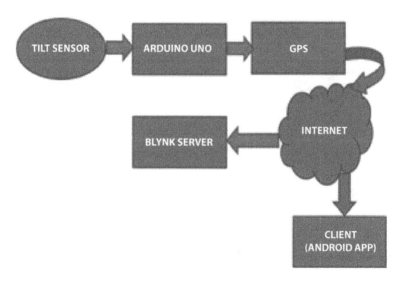

Figure 11.7 Flow chart for tilt sensor.

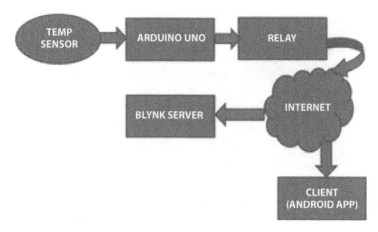

Figure 11.8 Flow chart of temperature sensor.

Here relay plays an important role to control the forest fire. The relay will activate the water pump which will immediately release water in the location to tackle the fire.

Figure 11.9 below shows the hardware output of the project.

This is the prototype that we will place in the forest area for anti-poaching purpose. The system consists of a buzzer which immediately alerts the surroundings when theft is happening (Figure 11.10). This prototype is connected to android application through Wi-Fi module and continuously transmits the data to the user. The software outputs are shown in Figure 11.5.

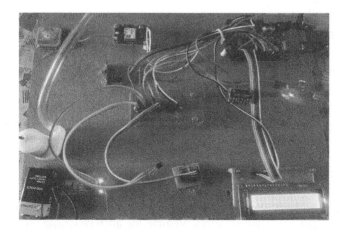

Figure 11.9 The proposed hardware prototype.

Figure 11.10 Forest prototype for display purpose.

11.5   Conclusion and Future Scope

This chapter has made a significant contribution to the field of wildlife safety systems, and it has been proposed using improvised methods. We saw the project as a journey on which we learned a lot of valuable lessons and gained new perspectives on the issue. We attempted to look at the problem from many perspectives, which resulted in the generation of some fresh ideas that could be investigated further in the future. The following are the project's principal applications:

- Detects anti-poaching activities accurately.
- Sends accurate GPS locations.
- Can control Wildfire scenarios.
- It can also be used for household purposes.

When it comes to the paper future scope, while the design was successful and developments such as GPS technology were developed, there are still enhancements that might be done in future versions. The future scope of work will include the implementation of a camera vision technology to track live footage when poaching occurs as well as a multi-node network and the incorporation of a microphone motion detector sensor to improve systems' ability to acquire data in the face of human or animal interference.

References

1. Joseph K. Paul, Tankala Yuvaraj, Karthikay Gundepudi, "Demonstrating Low-Cost Unmanned Aerial Vehicle for anti-Poaching", in 2021 *IEEE*

17th India Council InternationalConference (INDICON). DOI: 10.1109/INDICON49873.2020.9342131

2. Prasanti, K., Seelam, K., Jayalakshmi, C., & Savalam, C. S., "Preventive system for forests property using wireless communication" (2019). Preventive system for forests property using wireless communication. **2019**, *5ᵗʰ International Conference on Advanced Computing & Communication Systems (ICACCS).* DOI:10.1109/ICACCS.2019.8728514

3. P. G. Salunkhe, Poonam U. Chaudhari, "Design WSN Node for Protection of Forest Trees Against Poaching Based MSP430", **in 2018** *International Conference On Advances in Communication and Computing Technology* (ICACCT). DOI: 10.1109/ICACCT.2018.8529377

4. Mohan Sai S., Naresh K., RajKumar S.S., Mohan Sai Ganesh, Lok Sai, Abhinav, "An Infrared Image Detecting System Model to Monitor Human with Weapon for Controlling Smuggling of Sandalwood Trees", in 2018 *Second International Conference on Inventive Communication and Computational Technologies* (ICICCT). DOI: 10.1109/ICICCT.2018.8473140

5. Pratiksha Bhuta, Ajay Khandare and Rakhshan Anjum Shaikh, "Protocol Implementation for Wireless Sensor Network for Anti-Poaching of Trees", *IEEE WISPNET* 2017 conference. DOI: 10.1109/WiSPNET.2017.8299978

6. Anil Kulkarni, Ajay Khandare, Mandar Malve, "Wireless Sensor Network (WSN) for protection high-cost trees in remote jungles from fire and poaching", in 2014 *International Seminar on Sandalwood: Current Trends and Future Prospects.*

7. M. Sathishkumar, S. Rajini, "Smart Surveillance System Using PIR Sensor Network and GSM", 2015, *International Journal of Advanced Research in Computer Engineering & Technology* (IJARCET) Volume 4 Issue 1, pp. 45-76.

8. Prasad R. Khandar, K. Deivanai, "Preventive System for Forests" 2016, *International Journal of Computer Science Trends and Technology* (IJCST) – Volume 4 Issue 1, pp. 87-98.

9. Sarvesh Suhas Kapre, Saurabh Sahebrao Salunkhe, Rohan Manoj Thakkar, Akshay Prakash Pawar, and Omkar Ashok Malusare, "Advanced Security Guard with PIR Sensor for Commercial and Residential Use", 2014, *International Journal for Advance Research in Engineering and Technology* (IJARET) Volume 2, pp. 765-775.

10. Gaurav Kumar, Kusum Gurja & Shyam Babu Singh, "American Sign Language Translating Glove using Flex Sensor", 2016, *Imperial Journal of Interdisciplinary Research* (IJIR) Vol-2, Issue 6, pp. 456-461.

12

Tumor Detection Using Morphological Image Segmentation with DSP Processor TMS320C6748

T. Anil Raju[1*], K. Srihari Reddy[1], Sk. Arifulla Rabbani[1], G. Suresh[1],
K. Saikumar Reddy[1] and K. Girija Sravani[2†]

[1]Department of Electronics and Communication Engineering, Lakireddy Bali Reddy College of Engineering, Mylavaram, Krishna District, Andhra Pradesh, India
[2]Department of Electronics and Communication Engineering, KL University, Green Fields, Andhra Pradesh, India

Abstract

Image processing continues to enable the technology revolution that we are experiencing today. The main objective is to carry out a new cooperative approach for image segmentation and feature extraction using DSP Processor with good accuracy. The basic process involved in this paper to understand image segmentation is Edge detection. To improve the segmentation process and better estimation of the final clusters centers, involvement of DSP processor is used for computation and accuracy. Image segmentation using DSP processor TMS320C6748 is implemented in this proposed work. After detecting the edges of the image, Segmentation is done based on Morphological operations. The performance is measured by including some various optimization techniques and all results are shown using CCS platform. Hence our proposed method shows that the segmentation computation and accuracy is improved.

Keywords: Image segmentation, DSP processor TMS320C6748, thresholding method

*Corresponding author: anilrajulbrce123@gmail.com
†Corresponding author: kondavitee.sravani03@gmail.com

Abhishek Kumar, Suman Lata Tripathi, and K. Srinivasa Rao (eds.) Machine Learning for VLSI Chip Design, (185–194) © 2023 Scrivener Publishing LLC

12.1   Introduction

Image processing is an active research area which has become a vital component of a large number of present real-time applications. Segmentation is an important imaging technique for detecting abnormal changes in intensity levels of image. In computer vision, image processing is a highly challenging field; image segmentation is still a broad research topic and also an essential task in many applications because it plays a major role in the MRI image understanding. The MRI Images segmentation [1] has become the focus of contemporary research; some applications require a simple division of image into homogeneous regions while others require more accurate detection [2]. For this reason we need a special unit that we use for digital signal and image processing in a real-time execution and also the high-speed data transfer.

A digital signal processor [3] is one of the core technologies in rapidly growing application that become a key to many domains. Digital signal processors [4] such as the TMS320C6x family of Texas Instruments are like fast special-purpose microprocessors with a specialized type of architecture and an instruction set appropriate for signal processing. All the DSP methods are successful because of the combination of both hardware and software. The proposed algorithm will implement practically on our hardware.

12.2   Image Processing

12.2.1   Image Acquisition

MRI is a modern imaging technique that gives a more detailed image than CT scans and X-rays (Figure 12.1). MRI scans uses a large magnet field or radio waves to take images of the brain and other structures of the body. High spatial resolution and excellent soft tissue diagnosis are the advantages of MRI over other medical imaging techniques. In our research, the input MRI images are simulated with T1-weighted contrast and all images are obtained from the Brain web database from McConnell Brain Imaging Center of Montreal Neurological Institute at McGill University.

12.2.2   Image Segmentation Method

Segmentation is the division of an image into regions or categories which correspond to different objects or parts of objects [4]. Every pixel in an image is allocated to one of a number of these categories. It is an essential

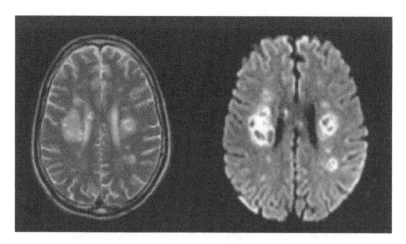

Figure 12.1 Brain MRI image.

step in image processing and also it is a critical stage of image. Image segmentation methods can be classified into three categories [5]: Edge-based, region-based, and pixel-based methods. Clustering and edge detection are important tools for a variety of medical applications.

12.3 TMS320C6748 DSP Processor

The processor which is going to be used is a TMS320C6748 DSP processor. This is a high-level processor which provides many features. It contains a 5v in power supply which will be given through an adaptor. It contains USB and OTG ports for connecting different devices. This board contains SATA (Serial Advances Technology Attachment) which is an interface for transferring the data between CPU and storage devices. A reset button is also present in this board for resetting the device.

An Ethernet port is also available for connecting to internet. This board provides some user buttons for the performing of different actions. The board is connected to a computer through JTAG. This board comes with a camera sensor through which we can capture images directly from the board. Along with camera sensor, a mic sensor is also present in this board through which we can take input speech signals directly. In accordance with these a fingerprint sensor is also available with this board which is only available in these versions. A VGA (video graphic array) port is also available through which we can connect the output to the display of the computer directly (Figure 12.2).

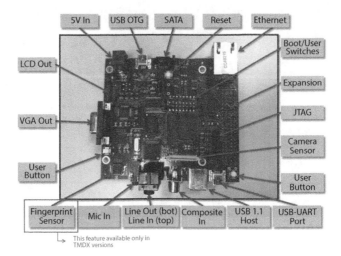

Figure 12.2 Texas instruments C6748 hardware development kit.

12.4   Code Composer Studio

Code composer studio software is an integrated development environment that supports Texas Instruments microcontrollers and embedded processors. Code composer studio software combines the advantage of eclipse software framework with advanced embedded and debug capabilities. There are some better features available in the Code Composer Studio. They are Program Code Editing, Application Building, and Application Debugging Features. CCS allows 'C' and Assembly language program. The Application Building Feature of the CCS is the basic process which is used to create, build, debug, and test the programs. The debugging features of CCS are loading data, FILE I/O, watch window, graphing signals, setting up of break points and usage of probe point. These languages save valuable time in the design process. The C and C++ code can be compiled as well as built to generate the desired file. The project we create keeps track of all the information regarding the input image we provided before preprocessing.

12.5   Morphological Image Segmentation

Thresholds in those algorithms may be decided on manually in step with a priori understanding mechanically through photograph information [6–14]. Algorithms may be in addition divided to facet-primarily based totally ones, region-primarily based totally ones and hybrid ones. Thresholds with inside the facet-primarily based totally algorithms are associated with the facet information. Structures are depicted via way of means of facet points. Common facet detection algorithms such as Canny facet detector and Laplacian facet detector may be categorised to this type. Algorithms try to locate facet pixels even as they get rid of the noise influence.

For example, Canny facet detector uses the brink of gradient value to locate the ability facet pixels and suppresses them through the tactics of the non-maximal suppression and hysterics shareholding. As the operations of algorithms are primarily based totally on pixels, the detected edges consist of discrete pixels and consequently can be incomplete or discontinuous. Hence, it is very important to use post-processing like morphological operation to attach the breaks or get rid of the holes. The technique has the cap potential to phase 3-d photographs with true accuracy; however, the drawback of this technique is the issue of the technique to system the photos of textured blob objects. This can be represented by the block diagram shown in Figure 12.3.

The proposed system has been developed to solve the problem of initial parameters for the level set algorithm such as the initial contour and its centre. Thresholding is a superb way to extract beneficial records encoded into pixels at the same time as minimizing heritage noise. This is performed

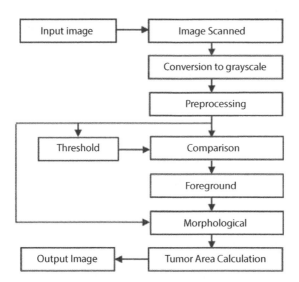

Figure 12.3 Proposed block diagram.

via making use of a remarks loop to optimize the edge fee earlier than changing the authentic grayscale picture to binary. The concept is to split the picture into parts, the heritage and foreground [6].

1. Select preliminary threshold fee, normally it imply 8-bit fee of the authentic picture.
2. Divide the authentic picture into portions:

   a. Pixel values which can be much less than or same to the edge; heritage (Background)
   b. Pixel values more than the edge; foreground

3. Find the common imply values of the two new images
4. Calculate the brand new threshold via averaging the two means.
5. If the distinction among the preceding threshold fee and the brand new threshold fee are beneath a distinct limit, the procedure is complete. Otherwise follow the brand new threshold to the authentic picture preserve trying.

The simplest property that pixels in a region can share is intensity. So the natural way to segment those intensities is through thresholding, the separation of light and dark regions. Thresholding creates binary images from grey-level ones by turning all pixels below some threshold to zero and all pixels about that threshold to one. (What you want to do with pixels at the threshold does not matter, as long as you are consistent.) If g(x, y) is a thresholded version of f(x, y) at some global threshold T,

$$g(x, y) = 1 \text{ if } f(x, y) \geq T,$$

$$g(x,y) = 0 \text{ otherwise.}$$

Morphology is nothing but the study of shape and structure of the image. Morphological image processing is a collection of non-linear operations related to the shape or morphology of features in an image. A morphological operation of a binary image creates a new binary image in which the pixel has a non-zero value only if the test is successful at that location in the input image.

12.5.1   Optimization

In order to improve the total execution time on the chip, various optimization techniques were used to check the performance: C code, CCS compiler and cache memory. The TMS320C6748 DSK provides a feature to change the size of cache memory from 0 KB to 256 K Bytes; it can be made by changing the parameters in the General Extension Language (gel file). The number of clock cycles required for each function is calculated and compared by a method called profiling for benchmark. In our methodology of profiling, all of its functions were analyzed and tested to determine the values of clock cycles. The improved performances were after adding the presented optimization technique.

To implement the Image Segmentation using code composer studio, the following steps are to be followed:

1. The C compiler accepts C source code and produces assembly language source code.
2. The assembler translates assembly language source files into machine language object files. The machine language is based on common object file format (COFF).
3. The assembly optimizer allows you to write linear assembly code without being concerned with the pipeline structure or with assigning registers. It assigns registers and uses loop optimization to turn linear assembly into highly parallel assembly that takes advantage of software pipelining.
4. The linker combines object files into a single executable object module. As it creates the executable module, it performs relocation and resolves external references. The linker accepts relocatable COFF object files and object libraries as input.
5. The archiver allows you to collect a group of files into a single archive file, called a library.
6. The archiver also allows you to modify a library by deleting, replacing, extracting, or adding members.
7. You can use the library-build utility to build your own customized run-time-support library.
8. The run-time-support libraries contain ANSI standard run-time-support functions, compiler-utility functions, floating-point arithmetic functions, and I/O functions that are supported by the C compiler.
9. The hex conversion utility converts a COFF object file into TI-Tagged, ASCII-hex, Intel, Motorola-S, or Tektronix object format. You can download the converted file to an EPROM programmer.

10. The cross-reference lister uses object files to cross-reference symbols, their definitions, and their references in the linked source files.

11. The absolute lister accepts linked object files as input and creates .abs files as output. You assemble the .abs files to produce a listing that contains absolute addresses rather than relative addresses. Without the absolute lister, producing such a listing would be tedious and require many manual operations.

12.6   Results and Discussions

In this section, some of the brain MRI images containing tumor taken for testing our proposed algorithm are shown below.

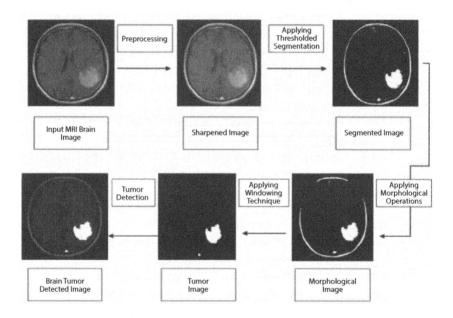

The results which are obtained by processing the image only by the software platform without involving hardware like DSP Processor is sensitive to noise. But results obtained by involving DSP Processor is not sensitive to noise and it improved the quality of classification (see Table 12.1).

Table 12.1 Performance improvement achieved.

n°	Function	Using optimization techniques	
		No. of CPU cycles (without optimization)	No. of CPU cycles (with optimization)
1	Image conversion	3924756	3131025
2	Median filter	91295273	73084236
3	Dividing original image	95877799	90436952
4	Average means of new images	3402892	2935339
5	Calculating new threshold	98642594	92527099
6	Comparing new and old threshold values	98623241	91348615
7	Obtaining output image after processing	93635675	89908543

12.7   Conclusions

This chapter proposed a powerful new approach for segmenting brain tumors and calculating their area using a Thresholding algorithm. The proposed method is tested on scanned MRI images of the human brain, and if there is noise, the non-uniformity is removed using a median filter and also by a modified new threshold value. The results show that the proposed approach to the detection of brain tumors may improve the quality of image segmentation and produce high diagnostic accuracy. Finally, you can make a rough deduction to calculate the shape of the tumor.

References

1. Koschan and M. Abidi. "Detection and Classification of Edges in Color Images", *IEEE Signal Processing*, **2021**, 18, pp. 256-262.
2. J. Canny, "A Computational Approach to Edge Detection", *IEEE Trans. Pattern Analysis and Machine Intelligence*, **2020**, 8, pp. 984-989.

3. G.T. Shrivakshan, Dr. C. Chandrasekar, "A Comparison of various Edge Detection Techniques used in Image Processing", *IJCSI International Journal of Computer Science Issues*, 2012, Vol. 9, Issue 5, pp. 567-573.

4. WenshuoGao, *et al.*, "An improved Sobel edge detection", Computer Science and Information Technology (ICCSIT), 2010, *3rd IEEE International Conference, China*, Volume 5, pp. 67-71.

5. Chen, L., "Laplacian Embedded Regression for Scalable Manifold Regularization", *IEEE Transactions on Neural Networks and Learning Systems*, **2015**, Vol. 23, pp. 902-915.

6. L. Chen, C. L. P. Chen and M. Lu, "A multiple-kernel fuzzy C-means algorithm for image segmentation," **2011**, Vol. 41, pp. 1263-1274.

7. Z. Chen, H. Yang, G. Zhang, and W. Shi, "Improvement and application of medical image segmentation method based on FCM," **2011**, Vol. 105, pp. 435-439.

8. B. Sharmila, N. Karalan, D. Nedumaran, "Image Processing on DSP Environment Using OpenCV," *IJARCSSE. Image Process.*, **2015**, Vol 5, pp. 489-493.

9. N. Kumar, S. Mahapatro, S. Pal, "Implementation of Color Image Enhancement using DCT on TMS320C6713," *IJECSE. Image Process.*, **2001**, Vol. 1, no. 3, pp. 1244-1253.

10. D. Zung, L.Pham, "Spatial models for fuzzy clustering", in *Computer vision and Image Understanding*, **2001**, Vol. 84, pp. 285-297, Elsevier Science (USA).

11. K. Honda, H. Ichihashi, S. Miyamoto, *Algorithms for Fuzzy Clustering Methods in c-Means Clustering with Applications*, Springer-Verlag, Berlin Heidelberg, **2008**, 23, pp. 56-65.

12. R.B. Dubey, M. Hanmandlu, Shantaram Vasikarla, "Evaluation of Three Methods for MRI Brain Tumor segmentation", *IEEE*, doi: 10.1109/ITNG.2011.92,2011.

13. Badiganti P.K., Peddirsi S., Rupesh A.T.J., Tripathi S.L. (2022) Design and Implementation of Smart Healthcare Monitoring System Using FPGA. In: Rawat S., Kumar A., Kumar P., Anguera J. (eds.) *Proceedings of First International Conference on Computational Electronics for Wireless Communications. Lecture Notes in Networks and Systems*, vol. 329. Springer, Singapore. https://doi.org/10.1007/978-981-16-6246-1_18

14. Vadla P.K., Naga Pawan Y.V.R., Kolla B.P., Tripathi S.L. (2021) Accurate Detection and Diagnosis of Breast Cancer Using Scaled Conjugate Gradient Back Propagation Algorithm and Advanced Deep Learning Techniques. In: Sengodan T., Murugappan M., Misra S. (eds.) *Advances in Electrical and Computer Technologies. Lecture Notes in Electrical Engineering*, vol 711. Springer, Singapore. https://doi.org/10.1007/978-981-15-9019-1_9

13

Design Challenges for Machine/Deep Learning Algorithms

Rajesh C. Dharmik* and Bhushan U. Bawankar

*Department of Information Technology, Yeshwantrao Chavan
College of Engineering, Nagpur, Maharashtra, India*

Abstract

Machine Learning, or ML, is one of the most effective uses of artificial intelligence because it allows systems to learn without having to be programmed regularly. A process of studying data for the purpose of constructing or training models occurs in Machine Learning. It has recently gained a lot of notoriety for its ability to be utilised across a wide range of businesses to solve difficult problems fast and effectively. Machine Learning has evolved into a quick and effective approach for businesses to construct models and strategize plans. It generates real-time results without the need for human intervention, using data that has already been processed. It develops data-driven models to make it easier to evaluate and interpret enormous amounts of data. Companies require software that can grasp data and produce correct outcomes, thus it is a skill in great demand. The main goal is to achieve optimal functionality with the least amount of confusion. Assuming you understand what machine learning is, why people use it, what different types of machine learning there are, and how the whole development pipeline works. What might potentially go wrong during the development process that would prohibit you from receiving accurate predictions? During the development phase, we are primarily concerned with selecting a learning algorithm and training it on some data; nevertheless, a faulty algorithm or bad data, or both, could be a problem. Despite the fact that there are countless cutting-edge apps produced utilising machine learning, there are some problems that an ML practitioner may face while developing an application from its inception to its final result. Poor data quality, underfitting of training data, overfitting of training data, lack of training data/insufficient training data/insufficient amount of training data, slow implementation, imperfections in the algorithm as data grows, irrelevant features,

---

Corresponding author: raj_dharmik@yahoo.com

Abhishek Kumar, Suman Lata Tripathi, and K. Srinivasa Rao (eds.) Machine Learning for VLSI
Chip Design, (195–210) © 2023 Scrivener Publishing LLC

non-representative training data, lack of quality data, making incorrect assumptions, becoming obsolete as data grows are some of the major challenges you may face while developing your machine learning model. To solve this problem, remove outliers from the training set, filter missing values, and remove unwanted features, increase the training time of the model, increase the complexity of the model, add more features to the data, reduce regular parameters, increase the training time of the model, analyse the data to the highest level of perfection, use data augmentation technique, remove outliers from the training set, and choose a model with fewer features.

Keywords: Machine learning, artificial intelligence, supervised algorithm, unsupervised algorithm, reinforcement learning algorithm

13.1   Introduction

Thanks to advancements in computer technology, through a computer network, we can now reserve and examine a huge quantity of data as well as retrieve it from physically different locations. Most of the equipment used to collect data is now digital. The data we see is explained by a process. We may be unable to fully identify the mechanism behind data production since we don't know the details, but we believe we can come up with a good approximation. The estimate may be able to account for some of the data. While we may not be able to identify the entire process, we can still recognize some patterns or regularities. This is where machine learning is at its best. Artificial Intelligence uses machine learning to improve the quality of applications. It enables systems to learn and comprehend information without the need to write new code for each new related behaviour. The goal is to automate the flow rather than constantly changing it. It generates real-time results without the need for human interaction, utilising data that has already been processed. It develops data-driven models to make it easier to evaluate and interpret enormous volumes of data. Machine Learning has evolved into a quick and effective approach for businesses to construct models and design plans [1].

Despite the fact that there are multiple cutting-edge apps produced utilising machine learning, there are certain problems that an ML practitioner may face while designing an application from the ground up and putting it to production. We shall go through some of the primary issues you can experience when building your machine learning model in this article. Assuming you understand what machine learning is, why people use it, what different types of machine learning there are, and how the whole development pipeline works. What might potentially go wrong throughout the development process that would prohibit you from receiving accurate predictions? Throughout the development phase, we concentrate on choosing a learning algorithm and training it on some data; the two factors that might cause a problem are a faulty algorithm or bad data, or both [2–4].

13.2   Design Challenges of Machine Learning

13.2.1   Data of Low Quality

Data is critical in the machine learning process. A shortage of high-quality data is one of the key issues that machine learning professionals face. Data that is unclear or noisy might make the whole process tedious. We don't want our system to make any wrong or erroneous predictions. As a result, data quality is essential for enhancing production. Obviously, your machine learning model will be unable to discover the right underlying pattern if your training data contains a substantial amount of mistakes, outliers, and noise. At end, it will perform poorly. A multitude of reasons can contribute to poor data quality, including:

- Noisy data can lead to inaccurate projections. As a result, classification accuracy suffers and output quality suffers. One of the most common data inaccuracies has been found.
- Incorrect or insufficient data can lead to erroneous programming in Machine Learning. With less data, the machine will analyse using only the most basic facts. The results are less precise because of this.
- Improving future actions requires the generalisation of earlier data input and output. However, one common issue is that the data generated is difficult to generalise.

At final, the data pre-processing procedure should be guaranteed and carried out to the possible standard including eliminating outliers, filtering missing values, and deleting unnecessary characteristics [3–6].

13.2.2   Training Data Underfitting

This occurs when data is unable to construct an accurate relationship between input and output variables. It basically entails attempting to squeeze into undersized pants. It means the data is too basic to form a definite link. When there isn't enough data to establish an accurate model, we use non-linear data to build or develop a linear model. If you use a linear model on a set with multi co-linearity, for example, it will almost certainly underfit and the predictions will be inaccurate on the training set as well. To solve this problem, increase the model's training duration, increase the model's complexity, add additional features to the data, reduce regular parameters, and increase the model's training time [3–6].

13.2.3   Training Data Overfitting

When a machine learning model is trained with a vast amount of data, it suffers from overfitting, and its performance worsens as a result. It is the equivalent of attempting to fit into a pair of large jeans. Unfortunately, this is one of the most significant challenges faced by machine learning professionals. This indicates that the algorithm was trained on erroneous and biased data, which will affect its overall performance. To help us understand, consider the following example. You went to a new city's eatery. You went to order anything from the menu but the price or bill was too high. You could think, "Eateries in the metro are so expensive and not cheap." Overgeneralizing is something we do all the time, and surprisingly enough, frameworks can fall into the same trap, which we call overfitting in AI. It indicates that the model is doing well on the training dataset, but it is not adequately generalised. In another, assume you're seeking to create and classify an Image Classification of apples, peaches, oranges, and bananas using training samples of 3500, 1500, 1500, and 1500, respectively. Because the number of training data for apples is much larger, the system is more likely to categorise oranges as apples if we train the model using these samples. Oversampling is the term used to describe this. To solve this problem, we may simplify the model by choosing one with fewer parameters, by minimising the amount of characteristics in the training data, limiting the model's capabilities, collect further training data, lower the volume, use data augmentation approach, remove outliers from the training set and analyze the data to the highest level of perfection [3–6].

13.2.4   Insufficient Training Data

Once the data has been obtained, you must determine whether the amount is adequate for the use case. Training the data is the most important duty in the machine learning process. Predicting will be biased if there is less training data. Using the acquired data, two crucial phases in a machine learning project are choosing a learning technique and training the model. As a result of our innate tendency to make mistakes, things may go wrong. The errors here might include choosing the incorrect model or picking inaccurate data. Let's look at an example to assist us to comprehend. Consider a machine learning system that is comparable to how a child is taught. You made the decision one day to educate a child about the difference between an apple and a watermelon. You will show him how to tell a watermelon from an apple. He will quickly grasp the knack of discriminating between the two in this manner. In contrast, a machine learning system takes a significant quantity of data to identify. Millions of data points may be necessary to solve difficult issues. As a result, we must make certain that machine learning algorithms are properly trained with relevant data [3–6].

13.2.5   Uncommon Training Data

To correctly generalise, the training data should be representative of new scenarios, i.e., the data we use for training should contain all examples that have occurred or will occur. When the training set is non-representative, it is unlikely that the model will make correct predictions. Machine learning models are systems that are meant to make predictions in the context of a business problem. Even though the model has never encountered data before, it will aid its performance. Sampling noise is unrepresentative data if the number of training samples is small, and if the training technique is faulty, numerous training tests cause sampling bias. Let's imagine you're trying to develop a model that can distinguish kinds of music. One method for constructing your training set is to conduct a YouTube search and use the results. We're assuming that YouTube's search engine is producing accurate results, but in fact, the results will be skewed toward popular musicians, maybe even artists in your area. So, when it comes to testing data, utilise representative data during training so that your model isn't skewed toward one or two classes [3–6].

13.2.6   Machine Learning Is a Time-Consuming Process

Machine Learning is a constantly evolving field. Fast subjective cost-benefit investigations are now in progress. Since the process is altering, the likelihood of making a mistake increases, in order to make learning more difficult. It involves data analysis, data bias removal, data training, and more. Another significant obstacle for Machine Learning experts is the fact that it is a very intricate procedure [3–6].

13.2.7   Unwanted Features

The machine learning system will not provide the desired results if the training data comprises a significant number of irrelevant features and not enough useful attributes. An important aspect for the success of machine learning is a Feature selection. Let's pretend, based on the data we gathered—age, gender, weight, height, and location—that we're working on a project to forecast how many minutes an individual wants to exercise.

1. Among these five characteristics, location value may have no bearing on our output function. This is an insignificant feature; we already know that we can achieve better outcomes without it.
2. We can also use Feature Extraction to combine two features to create a more useful one. By removing weight and height from our example, we can create a feature called BMI. On the dataset, we may also perform transformations.
3. Adding additional features by collecting more data is also beneficial [3–6].

13.2.8   Implementation is Taking Longer Than Expected

This is one of the most rare problems that machine learning experts face. Machine learning models take a long time to produce correct results. Slow programmes, data overload, and high requirements take a long time to produce reliable results. In order to get the optimum results, it needs continual monitoring and maintenance [3–6].

13.2.9   Flaws When Data Grows

So, you have acquired useful data, properly trained it, and your projections are extremely accurate. You've successfully created a machine learning algorithm! But wait, there's a catch: as data expands, the model can become obsolete. The current best model may become wrong in the future, necessitating significant reorganisation. You will need to check and maintain the algorithm on a frequent basis to keep it working. This is one of the most taxing problems that machine learning experts encounter [3–6].

13.2.10   The Model's Offline Learning and Deployment

When developing an application, machine learning engineers follow these processes: 1) Gathering data, 2) Cleaning data, 3) Feature development, 4) Pattern recognition, 5) Model training and optimization, 6) Implementation.

Oh! deployment? Yes, many machine learning practitioners do not have the skills for deployment. Due to a lack of experience and interdependence, a lack of grasp of the fundamental business models, a lack of awareness of business concerns, and volatile models, bringing their interesting apps into production has become one of the most challenging tasks. Data from websites such as Kaggle can be used to train a model. In actuality, we'll need to create a dynamically changing data gathering source. This sort of variable data may not be suitable for offline or batch learning. The system is trained before being put into production, where it continues to learn. As the data changes dynamically, it may wander. It is normally desirable to establish a pathway to harvest, analyse, implement or train, verify, and validate the dataset and train the system in batches for every machine learning project [5, 6].

13.2.11   Bad Recommendations

It's fairly common to use recommendation algorithms nowadays. Some may appear reliable, but others may fail to deliver. The recommendations of the proposal engines are susceptible to being imposed by machine learning. As a result, the advice will be ineffective if the outcome's requirement changes. When priorities vary, one of the most major issues with Machine Learning is that developing a complex algorithm, collecting massive amounts of data, and executing the process results in nothing but wrong results [5, 6].

13.2.12   Abuse of Talent

There aren't many specialists who can fully govern this technology despite the fact that many people are drawn to it. It is quite difficult to locate a skilled specialist that is capable of grasping Machine Learning issues and recommending a suitable software solution [5, 6].

13.2.13   Implementation

Combining newer machine learning algorithms with known procedures is a tough challenge. Maintaining good documentation and interpretation can help you get the most out of your resources. Machine Learning presents difficulties in terms of implementation [5, 6].

- Slow deployment – While Machine Learning algorithms are time efficient, the development process is not. Because it is still a novel concept, the implementation period has been extended.
- Data Protection – Retrieving confidential data on ML servers is risky because the machine won't be able to tell the difference between sensitivity and non-sensitivity [5, 6].

Storing sensitive data on ML servers is risky since the model won't be able to tell the difference between sensitive and non-sensitive data. A shortage of data was another important issue that arose during the model's development. Without enough data, it is impossible to deliver relevant information.

13.2.14   Assumption are Made in the Wrong Way

It is difficult for ML algorithms to handle misplaced data points. There should be a lot of missing data in the highlights. We may fill those empty cells instead of removing an element with a few missing attributes. The easiest method to trade with these Machine Learning problems is to make sure your data is complete and can convey a considerable quantity of information [5, 6].

13.2.15   Infrastructure Deficiency

Data stirring skills are required for machine learning. Inheritance frameworks are incapable of dealing with responsibility and are tense. Check to see if your infrastructure can handle Machine Learning difficulties. If it can't, you should aim to entirely update it with high-quality hardware and flexible storage [5, 6].

13.2.16   When Data Grows, Algorithms Become Obsolete

When taught, there will always be a large amount of data demanded. On certain data set, ML algorithms are trained to predict the future data and expect a same process with a large amount of data. At a moment where the data arrangement changes, the prior "correct" model over the data set may no longer be regarded as accurate [3, 4].

13.2.17   Skilled Resources are Not Available

Another issue with Deep Learning is that cognitive analytics and deep learning are still relatively new technologies in their current incarnations. Machine Learning professionals are necessary to maintain the process from the start coding to the maintenance and monitoring. Artificial Intelligence and Machine Learning are still new and to find manpower is a challenge. As a result, there is a scarcity of capable representatives to design and handle scientific ingredients for ML. Data scientists frequently need a mix of spatial knowledge as well as a thorough understanding of mathematics, technology, and science [3, 4].

13.2.18   Separation of Customers

Consider the data of a user's human behaviour throughout a testing period and the relevant historical practises. All things considered, an algorithm is required to distinguish between clients who will convert to a premium version of a product and those who will not. Based on the user's catalogue behaviour, a model with this choice issue would allow software to generate suitable suggestions for him [3, 4].

13.2.19   Complexity

Even though Machine Learning and Artificial Intelligence are growing in popularity, the majority of these areas are still in their infancy, relying mainly on trial and error. The technique is incredibly involved and time-consuming, from system setup to injecting intricate data and even coding. It is a time-consuming and difficult operation that does not allow for any blunders or errors [3, 4].

13.2.20   Results Take Time

The slow-moving software is another one of the most typical Machine Learning difficulties. Machine Learning Models require time to create, but they are very efficient and deliver precise results. The provision of findings takes longer than intended due to an abundance of data and requirements. This is due to the complicated methodology they utilise and the time it takes to provide usable results. Another factor is that it necessitates continuous monitoring throughout the process [3, 4].

13.2.21   Maintenance

Because the required outcomes for various activities are bound to vary, the data required for each is also bound to vary. This necessitates code modification as well as additional resources for monitoring changes. Regular monitoring and maintenance are required since the results must be standardised. The key to keeping the programme up to date is consistent maintenance [3, 4].

13.2.22   Drift in Ideas

This happens when the target variable changes, causing the given results to be incorrect. This causes the models to degrade since they are difficult to adapt to or improve. A model that can respond to a wide range of changes is required to solve this challenge [3, 4].

13.2.23   Bias in Data

When certain features of a data collection are more important than others, this occurs. Machine Learning Models frequently focus on certain properties inside the database in order to generalise the results. As a result, incorrect findings, poor outcome levels, and other problems occur [3, 4].

13.2.24   Error Probability

Biased programming will be present in many algorithms, resulting in biased datasets. It will not generate the desired results and will instead produce useless data. If it is used, it can lead to more serious flaws in business models. When the planning process isn't done correctly, this happens frequently. Machine Learning is all about short algorithms, as you've probably worked out by now. They need to identify the correct issue statement and develop a strategy before building the model. Machine Learning's biggest challenges stem from planning flaws prior to deployment [3, 4].

13.2.25   Inability to Explain

Machine Learning is sometimes referred to as a "black box" since understanding the results of an algorithm is often difficult and ineffective. This simply implies that the outputs are difficult to interpret since they are configured in unique ways to produce for specified situations. This lack of explainability makes algorithm reverse engineering almost hard, lowering the algorithm's trustworthiness [3, 4].

13.3   Commonly Used Algorithms in Machine Learning

Machine Learning algorithms are systems that can discover invisible patterns in data, predict output, and enhance performance based on their own experiences. Multiple algorithms can be used for different goals in machine learning. There are three types of machine learning algorithms:

A. Algorithms for Supervised Learning
B. Algorithms for Unsupervised Learning
C. Algorithm for Reinforcement Learning

13.3.1   Algorithms for Supervised Learning

Supervised learning is a type of machine learning in which machines are taught to predict outcomes using training data. The appropriate output has already been labelled with some input data. The training data presented to the computers is used to teach the machines to anticipate the output. When a student is learning under the guidance of their teacher, it uses the same principle. Supervised learning is the process of supplying input and proper output data to a machine learning model. A mapping function that maps the input variable to the output variable is the goal of a supervised learning program. In the real world supervised learning can be used for risk assessment, image categorization, fraud detection, and so on. In supervised learning, the model learns about each category of input using a labelled dataset. When the training phase is over, the model is evaluated and predicts the output. We have a variety of forms in the dataset. Each shape needs to be trained for the initial phase. The four sides of a square are the same length. If the form has three sides, it will be labeled a triangle. A hexagon is a six-sided shape having six equal sides. We use the test set to put our model to the test after training to determine whether it can recognise the form. The system has been trained on a variety of forms, and when it comes across a new one, it classifies it based on a variety of factors and predicts the outcome.

There are two sorts of challenges with supervised learning: regression and classification. Regression procedures are applied if there is a link between the input and output variables. It can be used to predict market trends and weather forecasts. Linear regression is a common supervised learning regression method. There are two classes, Yes-No, Male-Female, and True-False, when the output variable is categorical. Random Forest, Decision Trees and Logistic Regression are some supervised learning classification methods [8].

13.3.2   Algorithms for Unsupervised Learning

Unsupervised learning does not use a training dataset to supervise models. Patterns and insights that were previously unknown may be revealed by the information. The same thing happens in the human brain when learning. Unsupervised learning cannot be directly applied to a regression or classification job since, unlike supervised learning, we have the input data but no matching output data. Unsupervised learning tries to reveal the underlying structure of a dataset, categorise data based on similarities, and present the dataset in a compact manner. There is an input dataset with photographs of cats and dogs. The algorithm is never trained on the provided dataset, its characteristics are. The goal is to recognise visual characteristics on its own. The picture collection will be grouped based on visual similarity in order to complete the assignment.

Learning difficulties fall into two categories. Clustering is a method of grouping things together so that those who have the most in common stay in one group while those that have little or nothing in common stay in another. Cluster analysis discovers data object commonalities and categorises them based on their existence or absence. An association rule is a form of learning approach for discovering relationships between variables in a large database. There's a collection of objects that appear to be related. Marketing techniques are more effective when the association rule is used.

The list of several well-known unsupervised learning algorithms is Clustering with K-means, KNN (k-nearest neighbours), Clustering by hierarchy, Detecting anomalies, Principles of Neural Networks Analysis of Components, Analysis of Independent Components, Apriori and Decomposition of singular values [9].

13.3.3   Algorithm for Reinforcement Learning

Reinforcement Learning is a feedback-based Machine Learning technique in which an agent learns how to behave in a particular environment by performing actions and observing the results. For each outstanding activity, the agent receives positive feedback; for each terrible action, the agent receives negative feedback or a penalty. Unlike supervised learning, the agent learns on its own, based on feedback rather than tagged data. The agent can only learn from its own experience because there is no marked data. It's used to deal with issues when the decision-making is sequential and the goal is long term, such as games and robotics. On its own, the agent interacts with and explores the world. Assume you're in a labyrinth with an AI bot whose job is to find the diamond. The agent interacts with the environment by carrying out activities, and as a result of such actions, the agent's state is changed, as well as a reward or punishment as feedback. The agent learns and explores the world by performing action, changing state/remaining in the same state, and receiving feedback. The agent figures out which behaviours lead to positive feedback or rewards and which lead to negative feedback penalties. A good reward earns the agent a positive point, whereas a bad reward earns the agent a negative point. Q-Learning algorithm is used in reinforcement learning [10].

13.4   Applications of Machine Learning

In our daily lives we use machine learning without even realising it, for example, in Google Maps, Google Assistant, and Alexa. There are some popular Machine Learning applications.

13.4.1   Image Recognition

Machine learning can be used to recognize images. It can be used to identify people, locations, and digital photographs. To recognise a picture and identify a face is a general use of buddy tagging recommendation [7].

13.4.2   Speech Recognition

Speech recognition is a method for turning spoken instructions into text. Various voice recognition apps now employ machine learning methods [7].

13.4.3   Traffic Prediction

When we want to go somewhere new, we use the best and fastest route and anticipate traffic conditions. Machine learning employs two approaches to predict traffic conditions, such as whether traffic is clear, slow moving, or very crowded, by using Google Maps and sensors, which offer real-time car location while also using average time from prior days [7].

13.4.4   Product Recommendations

Machine learning is used by a number of e-commerce and entertainment companies, like Amazon, Netflix, and others, to deliver product suggestions to customers. Because of machine learning, once we search for a product on Amazon, we start seeing adverts for that product while surfing the web in the same browser. Google deduces the user's interests and offers items based on their choices using a number of machine learning algorithms. We utilise machine learning to discover suggestions, similar to how we use Netflix to find entertainment programmes, movies, and other stuff [7].

13.4.5   Email Spam and Malware Filtering

When we get a new email, we automatically sort it into three categories: essential, routine, and spam. Machine learning is the technology that allows us to get important communications with the important symbol in our inbox and spam emails in our spam box [7].

13.5   Conclusion

The system will not perform properly if the training set is too small, or if the data is not general, noisy, or contaminated with irrelevant properties. We went through some of the common issues that novices confront while learning to use machine learning. Machine learning is going to change the world. It has applications in medical diagnosis, voice recognition, product suggestions, video monitoring, and more. High compensation, good prospects, and job satisfaction are some of the benefits of this field. It is a high risk and reward technology. Before you start your machine learning adventure, make sure you thoroughly evaluate the obstacles listed above. You need to plan ahead, be patient, and put in your best effort to master this technology.

References

1. Ethem, Alpaydin, *Introduction to Machine Learning*. Second Edition; MIT Press, Cambridge, London, England.
2. Alex Smola, and S.V.N. Vishwanathan, *Introduction to Machine Learning*, Cambridge University Press.

3. https://www.geeksforgeeks.org/7-major-challenges-faced-by-machine-learning-professionals/
4. https://www.analyticsvidhya.com/blog/2021/06/5-challenges-of-machine-learning/
5. https://www.jigsawacademy.com/blogs/ai-ml/issues-in-machine-learning
6. https://towardsdatascience.com/top-8-challenges-for-machine-learning-practitioners-c4c0130701a1
7. https://www.javatpoint.com/applications-of-machine-learning
8. https://www.javatpoint.com/supervised-machine-learning
9. https://www.javatpoint.com/unsupervised-machine-learning
10. https://www.javatpoint.com/machine-learning-algorithms

About the Editors

Abhishek Kumar, PhD, is an associate professor at and obtained his PhD in the area of VLSI Design for Low Power and Secured Architecture from Lovely Professional University, India. With over 11 years of academic experience, he has published more than 30 research papers and proceedings in scholarly journals. He has also published nine book chapters and one authored book. He has worked as a reviewer and program committee member and editorial board member for academic and scholarly conferences and journals, and he has 11 patents to his credit.

Suman Lata Tripathi, PhD, is a professor at Lovely Professional University with more than 21 years of experience in academics. She has published more than 103 research papers in refereed journals and conferences. She has organized several workshops, summer internships, and expert lectures for students, and she has worked as a session chair, conference steering committee member, editorial board member, and reviewer for IEEE journals and conferences. She has published three books and currently has multiple volumes scheduled for publication from Wiley-Scrivener.

K. Srinivasa Rao, PhD, is a professor and Head of Microelectronics Research Group, Department of Electronics and Communication Engineering at the Koneru Lakshmaiah Education Foundation, India. He has earned multiple awards for his scholarship and has published more than 150 papers in scientific journals and presented more than 55 papers at scientific conferences around the world.

Index

Also of Interest

By the same editors

INTELLIGENT GREEN TECHNOLOGIES FOR SMART CITIES, Edited by Suman Lata Tripathi, Souvik Ganguli, Abhishek Kumar, and Tengiz Magradze, ISBN: 9781119816065. Presenting the concepts and fundamentals of smart cities and developing "green" technologies, this volume, written and edited by a global team of experts, also goes into the practical applications that can be utilized across multiple disciplines and industries, for both the engineer and the student.

DESIGN AND DEVELOPMENT OF EFFICIENT ENERGY SYSTEMS, edited by Suman Lata Tripathi, Dushyant Kumar Singh, Sanjeevikumar Padmanaban, and P. Raja, ISBN 9781119761631. Covering the concepts and fundamentals of efficient energy systems, this volume, written and edited by a global team of experts, also goes into the practical applications that can be utilized across multiple industries, for both the engineer and the student. *NOW AVAILABLE!*

Electrical and Electronic Devices, Circuits, and Materials: Technical Challenges and Solutions, edited by Suman Lata Tripathi, Parvej Ahmad Alvi, and Umashankar Subramaniam, ISBN 9781119750369. Covering every aspect of the design and improvement needed for solid-state electronic devices and circuit and their reliability issues, this new volume also includes overall system design for all kinds of analog and digital applications and developments in power systems. *NOW AVAILABLE!*

Green Energy: Solar Energy, Photovoltaics, and Smart Cities, edited by Suman Lata Tripathi and Sanjeevikumar Padmanaban, ISBN 9781119760764. Covering the concepts and fundamentals of green energy, this volume, written and edited by a global team of experts, also goes into the practical applications that can be utilized across multiple industries, for both the engineer and the student. *NOW AVAILABLE!*

Check out these other related titles from Scrivener Publishing

CONVERGENCE OF DEEP LEARNING IN CYBER-IoT SYSTEMS AND SECURITY, Edited by Rajdeep Chakraborty, Anupam Ghosh, Jyotsna Kumar Mandal and S. Balamurugan, ISBN: 9781119857211. In-depth analysis of Deep Learning-based cyber-IoT systems and security which will be the industry leader for the next ten years.

MACHINE INTELLIGENCE, BIG DATA ANALYTICS, AND IoT IN IMAGE PROCESSING: Practical Applications, Edited by Ashok Kumar, Megha Bhushan, José A. Galindo, Lalit Garg and Yu-Chen Hu, ISBN: 9781119865049. Discusses both theoretical and practical aspects of how to harness advanced technologies to develop practical applications such as drone-based surveillance, smart transportation, healthcare, farming solutions, and robotics used in automation.

MACHINE LEARNING TECHNIQUES AND ANALYTICS FOR CLOUD SECURITY, Edited by Rajdeep Chakraborty, Anupam Ghosh and Jyotsna Kumar Mandal, ISBN: 9781119762256. This book covers new methods, surveys, case studies, and policy with almost all machine learning techniques and analytics for cloud security solutions.

Printed and bound by CPI Group (UK) Ltd, Croydon, CR0 4YY

27/10/2024

14580125-0003